Love comes when you least expect it……

    Taggert Rhodes found out two things in one day….the first was that the father he never knew, had just died; the second, that Lily Fontaine was the about the prettiest lawyer he'd ever seen. Now he was thrust into a family he didn't know, and a lot of questions he needed to figure out the answers to. One thing was for sure though, Lily made all of those confusing things seem small in comparison to what just the sight of her, did to him.

    Lily Fontaine grew up knowing the Rhodes family, so, to find out that there was a son she never knew about, threw her for an emotional loop. She wasn't sure if she could trust him, but he made her feel things no other man ever could before. Could this handsome cowboy be the one person who made everything else in her life make perfect sense?

Lawyer Up, Cowboy

Book 3: Love As Big as Texas Series

Danette Fogarty

To horses, country music, and cowboys….

They make women feel romantic!

To my Fab 5 friends, thanks for the lunches and the breakfasts and the love and the conversation.

To Rachael, you helped me find Lily, I owe you one.

Chapter 1

The leather of the saddle creaked as Taggert adjusted himself into it. The west Texas sun was high and bright today, making the sweat trace lines down his back. Even with his well-worn cowboy hat providing some shade, the heat still permeated his face. His mount, a brown stallion named Diego, moved restlessly beneath him.

"I know," Taggert crooned to the horse, "I want to go too."

They stood, man and horse, upon a ridge that overlooked a field. The view spanned miles, as far as the eye could see, and contained a lot of cattle.

This part of Texas was where the rolling hills, dotted with rocky outcroppings, met with the dry grasslands. Eventually, a hundred miles or so down the road, the lands flattened into a more desert-like landscape.

Taggert scanned the area, watching for stray cattle in the dense tree lines that dotted the area. If a small calf got stuck or a mama wandered, it was Taggert's job to notify one of the cowboys so they could wrangle the straggler.

The smell of open spaces, worn leather, and horse filled his nostrils. Feeling the slight breeze move across his cheek gave Taggert a sense of freedom.

"Someday," he patted the horse's neck, "we'll have our own spread and we'll have our own herd."

Hearing the crackle of his radio, he listened to the men as they approached his location with the herd of cattle.

With over a thousand head of cows coming his way, he knew things could be difficult if the cowboys lost the upper hand.

Taggert watched closely as the main part of the herd passed him by. Another cowboy raised his hat in a wave to let Taggert know they were doing well.

When the last of the cowboys and cows were passed his position, he scanned the pasture one last time before turning to head in the direction of the herd. He would ride ahead and find yet another perch and do the same thing. As the most experienced cowhand, it was his responsibility to get the others situated while making sure his boss' investment was protected.

As he came down the incline to the main pasture, Taggert noticed a vehicle coming toward him.

It was moving at a fast pace, which made him frown.

"Who in the Sam Hill is that?" he asked to no one.

Staying right where he and his horse stopped, Taggert waited for the vehicle to approach. Whoever it was, they were sure in a hurry.

He recognized the ranch's jeep and wondered why they would send someone out. It wasn't unheard of, but the foreman and the owner both trusted Taggert to do what needed to be down without micro-managing.

The jeep stopped about fifteen feet away from where he and Diego were standing.

Legs were the first thing Taggert saw as she stepped out of the jeep. Legs that were long and attached to high heels. His eyes travelled upward and rested on a shapely figure in a dark blue skirt with a matching suit jacket.

Not moving, Taggert watched her walk over to him. The rocky, uneven ground didn't seem to bother her, even in the heels. That was impressive, but nothing as impressive as the face that belonged to that body; that...was intense.

She was tall for a woman; he'd wager maybe five foot, seven. And she was solid, not big, but he could see that she either worked out or knew her way around a ranch. She didn't seem at all intimidated by walking up to a man who sat on a horse that was over seventeen hands tall.

Her hair was a dark brown, almost black. It came down past her shoulders and curled a little at the ends. The breeze took it and played with it, distracting Taggert's eyes before he focused fully on her face. When he did make eye contact, he noticed she had beautiful blue eyes that reminded him of a clear stream flowing through the countryside.

"Mr. Taggert Rhodes?" Lily Fontaine asked, her hands planted on her hips.

Taggert tipped his hat in greeting, "That's what my momma said," he answered, a grin breaking his face.

Lily was not amused, "I'm here to inform you that your father, Ken Rhodes, passed away, and you are in his will." She took a step closer and stuck out her arm, an envelope in her hand for him to accept.

Reaching forward, Taggert took the envelope. He looked at it for a moment, confused, then looked back up. In that short amount of time, she closed the distance to the jeep and was getting in.

Sitting there on his horse, Taggert wondered what just happened.

Lily Fontaine sat in the jeep on the ride back to the ranch, scowling.

Not only did she drive all the way past San Antonio to this little town in west Texas, but she had to make a rather uncomfortable hour-long jeep drive to where this Taggert Rhodes was.

The jeep bumped along, making her teeth rattle. She wasn't wearing appropriate clothing for this ride, but she was dressed for work so she had to go with it. When she spoke to the foreman of the ranch, he directed her to where this

Taggert man was and she hopped in the jeep, not thinking of how uncomfortable the ride would be.

'But it's done,' she thought to herself. She'd delivered the copy of the information to him, along with a letter from Ken.

Thinking back to the week before, she was still reeling emotionally.

When Ken Rhodes went to the hospital after a heart attack, her mother contacted her.

As the family attorney, Lily was responsible for all legal matters regarding the Rhodes family. After all, her father was good friends with Ken Rhodes, and she, in effect, grew up with Ken Jr. and Seth. They were like her older brothers and taught her how to ride as soon as she could figure out how to get on a horse.

Smiling for the first time in days, Lily relished those memories. Ken Sr. was the one who first introduced her to her first horse.

Shaking herself out of those cozy thoughts, she realized that this wasn't the point. The point was, that she didn't know Ken Sr. at all, apparently.

When Ken Sr. was pronounced brain dead the following morning, the family waited for everyone to say good bye before taking him off of life support.

The situation was traumatic and Lily was there with Seth and Ken Jr. and their families.

She sat with the boys and their wives until Ken Sr. was gone and then went back to her office to start the legal end of things.

It was only after she found the file for Ken Sr.'s estate that she was blind-sided for the first time.

Reading the will, she found it was straight forward. Ken's wife, Rachael, would retain the house they currently owned after retiring from the ranch and would have a portion of the estate for her use. The rest would be divided up between Ken's children: Ken Jr., Seth, and Taggert Rhodes.

As soon as her eyes scanned the name, Taggert Rhodes, Lily was flabbergasted. Who the hell was Taggert Rhodes?

She immediately called her mother, demanding answers. After all, she couldn't very well go knocking on Rachael Rhodes' door after she just lost her husband and ask about a son no one had ever mentioned before.

Her mother asked her to stay put and came over.

Lily sat there, in her office, and listened to a story that, even now, she couldn't quite digest.

The fact was, Ken Sr. had a third son that no one knew about except Ken and her father. The only reason Lily's mother knew was because her father mentioned it briefly many years earlier.

Taking in the information had actually been the easiest part of it all. After that, things really got complicated.

As the attorney of the estate, she usually didn't discuss will "issues" until the reading, and that was usually after the funeral. Only now, this involved a family member that no one knew about, and maybe Taggert himself wasn't aware of the situation.

In the interest of the estate, Lily knew she not only had to find this Taggert Rhodes, but she would be the one to break the news to Rachael and her sons. That was not something she was happy about doing.

The day after Ken Sr. passed away, she called Rachael and asked if she could come over and speak to the family. Rachael said, "of course."

When she arrived at Seth and Raelynn Rhodes' house, it was packed with family.

Lily put on her best "lawyer" face and went inside. She offered her condolences to the extended family and then asked Rachael, Seth, and Ken Jr. to come into Seth's office.

They sat down, puzzled by the request; Lily didn't even know where to begin. She was relieved when Rachael spoke first.

"This is about Taggert, isn't it?" she asked Lily.

Seth looked at his mother, "Who is Taggert?" he asked her.

Looking directly at her sons, Rachael answered, "He's your brother."

Being the observer, Lily thought that the brothers handled the news very well, considering the circumstances. There were, of course, the usual "What the..?" questions and voices were filled with emotion.

Finally Rachael calmed them all down, tears streaming down her face. "Your father was still in his rodeo days, you boys know that," she started. "I think he was lonely and met a woman there." She put up her hand when Ken Jr. tried to interject, "Taggert was the result of a very short relationship and both your dad, and the woman involved, agreed that he would not have an active role in Taggert's life." She looked at her sons, her face filled with emotional pain. "I asked your father to tell you years ago but he always said there was plenty of time." She dabbed her eyes with a tissue, "I think he was afraid."

"Afraid of what?" Seth asked his mother.

Rachael answered, "Afraid of what you boys would think of him," she looked at Lily, "afraid of what others would say about him going out on me."

Lily nodded; she understood the small town mentality very well. Three decades earlier, that kind of thing would have shaken his very standing in the community.

Being jolted back to the present by the jeep jumping from dirt to a gravel drive, Lily thought about what was said that day.

If everything she was told was accurate, and she believed it was, then even Taggert wasn't aware of his father, or the money the estate contained.

Looking around, she missed the green pastures surrounding Alvin, Texas, her hometown. Out here, it seemed so....desolate.

As soon as the driver got her back to the main ranch, Lily thanked both him, and the foreman, for their time. She got into her car and on the main road back toward Houston in record time.

The next few days were going to be very interesting indeed.

Taggert didn't open the envelope right away. He tucked it into a pouch on his saddle and waited until everyone was settled down for the night. Being the most senior cowhand, he, at least, got his own room. The others shared a large bunkroom in the same building.

He sat on the bed and opened the envelope. Inside, he found a letter.

After taking off his boots, he slid up the bed and leaned against the headboard. The paper was crisp as he unfolded it between his fingers.

It read:

Taggert:

I hope this letter finds you well. I'm sure if you're reading this, it means I'm gone. It was my fervent wish that we meet but I'm not sure I have the bravery I would need in order for that to happen. Not that I regret you, your mother has been very kind in keeping me apprised of your schooling and general health over the years. My only contribution was paying for your education and extra-curricular activities; far from being a proper father but your mother and I decided it was best that way.

If you did not meet me, then I would like to say that I lived my life the best I could. I loved only one woman, Rachael, who gave me two sons, Ken Jr. and Seth. They are good men and I hope that you will appreciate that. Your mother, as she explained to me, has told you of our meeting and your birth as a result. I always thought she was a kind and generous woman. I assume she raised you to be the same.

It is to that attribute that I beg your forgiveness for not being an active part of your life, and for not letting you have time growing up with your brothers.

I have done well in my business endeavors and would like to acknowledge your legitimacy as one of my heirs. You will receive an equal share of my estate with your brothers. Perhaps this will, in some small way, make up for the years we missed.

If your mother has never told you this, I will say, I loved you from the moment you were born. You may not understand that, but it's true.

If you choose not to meet your brothers, I will understand, and I know they will too. However, if you choose to know them, please, take the time to let them get to know you. There is so little time and we all tend to take it for granted.

Love,

Your Father,

Ken Rhodes

Taggert read the letter three times before setting it on the nightstand next to his bed. It only created more questions than it answered.

A tornado of emotions swam through Taggert; the first being confusion, the last being anger. He was angry that he never met the man who was his father. Even more, he was angry that his mother kept in touch with Ken Rhodes when she always told Taggert that she didn't know where he was.

Picking up the phone, Taggert dialed his mother's number. She picked up right away.

"This is about Ken, isn't it?" his mother, Claire, asked without preamble.

Hearing the hurt in his mother's voice took a bit of the steam from his anger, but only a bit. "Yes, it is," he answered. "When were you going to tell me?" Taggert blurted out the question.

Claire Walden had been sitting in her apartment, crying for hours before her son's call. She'd been contacted by a lawyer named Fontaine, who wanted her son's contact information. When the lawyer told her that Ken was dead, it hurt, more than she ever thought it would.

"I don't know," she finally replied, her voice soft and thick with tears.

Glancing over at the letter on the nightstand, Taggert's eyes focused on the words, 'Your Father,' and told his mother, "I'm going."

Chapter 2

Lily sat in her office the next day, feeling irritable and restless. Tomorrow was the funeral for Ken Rhodes Sr. and she was still trying to deal with what, she felt, was a betrayal.

Growing up, the two men she admired the most were her father and Ken Sr. They were big, strong, immortal figures in her mind and all that seemed like a big, fat illusion now.

When her father retired a couple of years earlier, he came to Lily and asked her to take over the practice. She'd been working in Houston for a small firm then and was pretty happy. She didn't work on high-profile cases and certainly wasn't making a million dollars, but she felt like she was doing some good.

Remembering his visit, she tried to keep from crying. He'd walked into her office and sat down, looking nervous. In her whole life, she never remembered her father, the great Maxwell Fontaine, Esquire, look nervous.

"Lily," he said with a weak smile, "I'm asking you to come home and run the practice."

She was confused at the time because he never once mentioned retirement. Instead, she got up, a look of worry on her face, and walked around her desk to sit next to him, before asking, "Why, Dad?"

"It's time," he answered.

They both knew at the time that his answer wasn't the whole truth. But, without thinking about it, Lily answered, "Sure, Dad."

Two months later, she was working full time beside her father, going over things that a small town attorney would need to know.

It wasn't as face-paced as her job in Houston, but she liked the work. Most of the people who came in were people she, or her dad, knew. There was a kind of comfort in that.

That time was a happy one, until her father fell ill at work one day.

She'd gone over to her parents' house, picked up her mother, and they went to see him at the hospital and were told that he had cancer. As if that wasn't bad enough, he'd known about it for months and hadn't told either her or her mother.

Within weeks, he was gone.

Lily really thought she'd laid that feeling of betrayal to rest in her mind and heart, but now, with this whole thing with Ken Sr., she wasn't so sure.

Her thinking was interrupted by her assistant, Jennifer, "Ms. Lily," the younger woman said, "I have a Mr. Taggert Rhodes on the phone for you."

The term, "Speak of the Devil," had new meaning now in Lily's mind. Taggert Rhodes was the "devil" right now in her way of reasoning.

"Mr. Rhodes," she said in a brusque voice, "How can I help you?"

Taggert smiled into the phone. Oh, this Lily Fontaine was like one of the wild horses he'd seen. You were sure afraid they'd take off your hand if you put it too close. He had the exact same feeling from Ms. Fontaine. Now was not the time to compare his father's lawyer to a wide animal, so he answered, "I'd like to meet my brothers and Mrs. Rhodes."

His answer left Lily momentarily stunned. "I'm sure I can arrange something," she countered when she regained use of her mind. "When would be good for you?"

"Today," Taggert said. He was calling her from his hotel room, here in Alvin.

Her mind spinning, Lily debated for a few seconds, then said, "Okay, why don't you meet me at the ranch in about two hours; that will give me time to get the family together."

Nodding, Taggert only said, "That's fine," and hung up.

Looking at her phone, Lily seethed. If she wasn't so emotionally invested in this family, none of this would be so difficult. Logically, she knew that, but emotionally, she wanted to punch someone square in the face!

She picked up her cell phone and called Rachael Rhodes.

Two hours later, Taggert was driving down FM 1462, just outside of Alvin. It was a nice area, he thought, as he drove through. Small enough that there was space as soon as you left the town, but there were conveniences nearby.

He slowed down his truck to make the turn into the driveway, marked with the gate that read Rhodes Ranch.

The driveway was a long one, surrounded by green pastures on either side. He saw the house and smiled; it was a large cabin style, but newer, he noticed.

In all of his daydreams about his father, Taggert never pictured him living on a ranch. For some reason, he always thought of his father as some big business mogul who travelled the world. Now, the truth was right in front of him.

He pulled up and parked next to the other vehicles, just to the right of the house. He got out in time to see Ms. Fontaine come out of the house, followed by a man and a woman.

Absently running his hands down his jeans, to make sure they were dry, Taggert shut the door and turned around.

"Taggert," Lily nodded, "this is your brother, Seth, and his wife, Raelynn."

Whatever Taggert expected when he met his brother never prepared him for the reality of it.

Seth smiled, stepped forward, and put his hand out, "Taggert," he said as if he were trying out the name on his lips.

Extending his hand, Taggert took his brother's in his firmly.

"Taggert," Raelynn said, smiling, "welcome." She stepped forward and hugged her brother-in-law.

Not knowing what to do, Taggert returned her hug. Emotions moved through him that he couldn't name at the moment.

Lily stood there, shocked by Seth and Raelynn's reaction to Taggert.

Pulling back, Raelynn smiled and said, "Please, come inside."

The four of them moved to go inside.

Once in the entrance of the house, Taggert's nerves reared up again.

Lily took on the role of introductions once again. She led Taggert into the great room and held on to his arm as she went, "Taggert, this is your brother, Ken Jr., his wife, Charlotte, and their youngest kids, Tyler and Becky. They have two more, Amy and Ken III, but they're older and couldn't come due to school conflicts." She turned and smiled as the housekeeper brought a squirming little girl, around three years of age, toward them, "This spitfire is your niece Hannah. She is Seth and Raelynn's daughter."

Standing there, Taggert wasn't sure what to say. He watched little Hannah wiggle out of the woman's arms and head right for him. She was a bundle of energy with blonde curls and bright blue eyes.

Hannah looked up at him and said, "Ucle Agger."

Everyone laughed.

Nodding, Taggert bent down so he could be on the little girl's level. "I'm your Uncle Taggert," he said and almost fell backward when she flung herself into his arms.

Lily almost fell over in shock. She looked over at Raelynn and Seth, who looked as surprised as she was. Hannah was not known for her warmth towards strangers. She was extremely particular about who she "liked." The fact that she was plainly enamored by her "Uncle" was surprising, to say the least.

Taggert tried to put Hannah down, but she only hung on tighter. Figuring she was like most women, with a mind of her own, he simply held her as he shook Ken's hands, then his wife's. He nodded to their kids, who smiled in return.

They were going to sit down when another woman entered the room. Taggert looked over and knew, somehow, that this was his father's wife, Rachael. She was beautiful, obviously grieving, given the bruises under her eyes, but still beautiful.

Rachael walked over to where Taggert stood, holding Hannah. If Hannah already liked him, then they would all, in time. "Taggert," she said softly and touched his arm with her hand, "welcome."

The emotions built up again and Taggert wasn't sure what to do with them. All of these strangers were treating him like he'd been there his whole life. It was surreal.

Raelynn walked over and took a, not pleased, Hannah from Taggert. She looked at Tyler and Becky and asked them to take Hannah into the kitchen for a snack. Mrs. Bentler would take care of them.

"Everyone sit, please," Rachael said.

They sat down, with Ken, Charlotte, Seth, and Raelynn on one sofa, and Taggert on the other. Rachael sat on one side of him while Lily Fontaine was on the opposite side.

Rachael spoke first, "Can we get you anything to drink, Taggert?"

He shook his head and answered, "No, ma'am, I'm fine, thank you."

Lily thought, 'At least he has manners,' then shushed her inner voice.

"Well," Rachael said, "you requested this meeting so I'm sure you have questions." She looked over at her boys and smiled, "So shoot. I'll answer honestly to the best of my ability."

Just having met her minutes before, Taggert knew that Rachael Rhodes would do just that.

"I guess," he said, nodding to her, "my first question is, did you know about me?"

Rachael looked directly at him, "I did, yes, but your brothers did not before last week."

He looked over at Seth and Ken Jr, and asked them, "Why do you think he didn't tell you?"

The brothers exchanged glances and then looked back at Taggert; Seth explained, "We've asked ourselves that same question, Taggert."

Ken interjected, "I personally think he was so used to having you separate that he just didn't know how to face up to it."

Taggert nodded, "Were you mad when you found out?" he asked Seth and Ken.

Lily wasn't sure what she expected from this "meeting," but this wasn't it.

"Honestly," Seth responded, "I think we were just shocked. Mom actually told us before Lily could."

Looking over at Lily Fontaine, Taggert studied her for a moment. She exuded business, but there was something underneath all of that, anger maybe, that he couldn't quite place.

"Are you mad now?" he asked his brothers.

Ken leaned forward, his hands clasped between his knees, "I'm not mad but I can't speak for Seth." He frowned, "honestly, I'm disappointed that he didn't think any of us could handle it."

Seth nodded, "That's about it for me too, I suppose."

Rachael looked at all three of Ken's sons and felt a tremendous amount of sadness as a tear slipped down her cheek, "If he could see the three of you now, and I'm sure he can, then he would regret that."

Seth was about to stand, when Rachael put up her hand to let him know she was okay. "I'm fine." She smiled, then took Taggert's hand into hers, "You are a Rhodes, Taggert. We all have questions, but that is the fact of it. You are welcome here."

Lily felt tears sting her own eyes. Inside, she knew this was what Ken Sr. would've wanted. It didn't dull the pain of her response to the lies but it was certainly a start.

"Thank you, ma'am," Taggert answered her, and squeezed her hand.

Mrs. Bentler came into the room, "I have lunch prepared out on the patio if you'd all like to come out."

Everyone stood and Taggert waited until the others preceded him before moving. He needed just a moment to collect his feelings.

Lily was almost to the hallway, leading to the kitchen, when she noticed Taggert was still standing near the sofa in the living room.

"Are you okay, Mr. Rhodes?" she asked.

Turning to look at her, Taggert had to suck in a breath. She was prettier than a pony running through the pasture in west Texas. Finding his voice, he answered, "Taggert, please, ma'am, and I'm just fine."

Walking over to where he stood, Lily studied his face. He was actually very handsome, not that she'd ever admit that. He was as tall as his brothers, just over six feet, but his hair was dark brown, where theirs was light brown. His eyes were brown, where both Seth and Ken Jr. had blue eyes. She supposed that was passed on from his mother.

As he looked at her, she felt like he was internally dismantling her, trying to figure her out. Since she couldn't even do that herself, she doubted he'd get anywhere with that. But it was sure nice to have a man look at you that way.

"Well, Taggert," she said, to break the tension that seemed to manifest out of nowhere, "why don't we join the others for lunch?"

Taggert looked at Lily Fontaine, and found, he wanted to kiss her. Not the peck on the cheek kind, or Sunday after church greeting kind, but the deep, lose yourself in the magic of discovering someone's lips kind.

He held out is arm to Lily. When she took it, he smiled, and they walked toward the kitchen.

30

Lawyer Up, Cowboy

Chapter 3

An hour later, it was if Taggert had been a part of the family forever. They spoke of funny things, the trouble the three boys got into as kids, the stories Seth and Ken Jr. told about their own children.

It amazed Taggert, that even in the midst of loss, this family was able to see the good in things, and that laughter could still be found.

Rachael raised her glass, "I'd like to make a toast," she waited for everyone to raise theirs before saying, "to reunions. Even though long overdue, we'll all find that it's never too late."

Tipping his glass against his sister-in-law's, Raelynn, Taggert wondered if Rachael was speaking about him, or his father.

Ken Jr. had been quiet through most of the lunch, adding a story here and there, but mostly just listening. He looked over at Taggert and said, "Now, I'm getting mad at him."

Everyone was quiet, not sure what to say to the statement.

"I mean, this could have been all of us." He looked at his mother, and asked, "He never told you why?"

Rachael shook her head to answer no. "The last time we spoke about it was just after Lily's father past away a couple of years ago."

Taggert's eyes darted to where Lily sat, looking down at her plate.

Seth asked, "What did he say?"

"When we spoke about it, he said that it was high time he realized he needed all three of his boys with him." Rachael barely got out the words before getting choked up.

Feeling awful for hurting his mother, Seth whispered, "I'm sorry, Mom."

Smiling, Rachael answered, "Don't be." She looked from Seth, to Ken Jr., and then to Taggert. "None of you have anything to be sorry for. It was your father's fault for not making choices sooner." She looked back at Taggert, "And you'll never know what kind of man he was."

Not sure if he should speak about it, Taggert responded, "I'm certainly not trying to insult you, Miss Rachael, but my momma always spoke highly of him."

Another tear slipped down Rachael's cheek, "I'm so glad."

This was a complicated situation and none of them knew how to navigate the complicated emotional minefield it created.

"Speaking of your mother," Rachael said to Taggert, "Is she coming to the funeral tomorrow?"

Lily's eyes shot up to Mrs. Rhodes. By the look on her son's faces, they were just as shocked by the question.

Taggert wasn't sure how to answer so he just shook his head.

Rachael sighed, "Well, please tell her that she is welcome to come. I know that she kept in touch with your father, so she must be feeling that loss as well."

Astounded, Lily merely stared. What an extraordinary family the Rhodes family was! Love was what mattered. She knew her mother and father loved her, but it wasn't as open as it was for Seth and Ken Jr., and now Taggert. She felt a tinge of envy for them.

"Thank you, ma'am, I'll pass that on." Taggert answered.

Mrs. Bentler had just come out to start clearing dishes when Raelynn stood to help her. "Rachael," she said to her mother-in-law, "why don't you and the boys take Taggert inside and show him some of the pictures from the family photo albums?"

Rachael nodded and led the way inside, Seth, Ken Jr., and Taggert following her.

Charlotte sighed, "I think that our mother-in-law is a special kind of woman," she said to Raelynn.

"I agree," Raelynn smiled. She looked over to Lily, and asked, "Are you okay?"

Knowing that Raelynn could read people easily, she probably picked up on the fact that the mention of Lily's father would make her sad. She smiled at her friend, and picked up some dishes, "I'm fine, but thank you for asking."

They all walked inside and deposited dishes onto the counter. Raelynn started washing, Lily dried, and Charlotte put them away. No one really talked; they were still mulling over the situation with Ken Sr.

After the dishes were done, Raelynn peeked into the Great Room to see how the boys and Rachael were doing.

Rachael was sitting on one of the sofas, Seth was on one side, Taggert on the other side, and Ken Jr. was behind her, bent over so he could see the pictures.

Seeing them like this, Raelynn could see the resemblance between the brothers. Taggert may have darker coloring, but he was a Rhodes, through and through.

The thoughts made her happy and sad at the same time. It would probably always be like that, the dichotomy of the situation Ken Sr. created.

She did see that her husband seemed fine and that was what was important to Raelynn. Losing his father was a blow and, even though Ken Sr. and Rachael retired up north, they still spoke to Seth weekly on the phone. From what Charlotte told her, it was the same way with Ken Jr. The saving grace in this was Rachael. She was a strong woman and would do whatever her sons needed. Right now, it seemed that they needed to understand Taggert's role in their family.

Lily came up behind Raelynn and gently touched her shoulder.

When Raelynn turned around, she was smiling, but there were tears welling up.

"Are you okay?" Lily asked, worried.

Raelynn nodded, "Yes. Just feeling sentimental, I guess."

Not at all sure what her friend meant, Lily smiled in return and went back into the kitchen.

She sat down at the table next to Charlotte, and Raelynn sat across from them.

Feeling funny about asking, but wanting to know, Lily asked them, "Are the two of you mad about what's going on?"

For Raelynn, who'd lost a husband years earlier, it was a little more complicated. She tried to explain, "When Anthony died, I was lost, truly, lost." Smiling, she added, "But then I found out about Hailey and it was like a way for Anthony to make sure I had someone to love and help me through it."

She looked toward the great room, hearing the murmur of the boys' voices, mixed with Rachael's, and sighed. "Taggert is their Hailey."

It seemed way too easy for them, at least in Lily's eyes. They were her friends and she was angry for them. "I don't know if I could just welcome some long, lost sibling into the mix," she said.

Charlotte smiled, "But you didn't have Ken Sr. or Rachael either." She could see Lily's defensiveness and added, "I know your parents and they are lovely people. I'm just saying that there is some sort of inherent kindness, especially in Rachael."

That fact was something Lily could definitely agree with. Lily had never met anyone quite like Rachael Rhodes. The boys were lucky to have her. Lily made a mental note to see her own mother soon and let her know how much she was appreciated.

"Dad never was big on communication," Lily announced dryly, and the three of them laughed.

Just then, there was a ruckus and the back door opened up to a very wound up Hannah, coming into the kitchen.

She looked at the women and frowned, "Mama, where Ucle Agger?" she asked.

Chuckling, Raelynn got up and went over to pick up her, now very dirty, daughter. "He's busy with Nana and Daddy and Uncle Ken so you'll have to wait a little bit."

Hannah took a moment to digest the information and then let out a wail, "I want Ucle Agger!" she yelled.

As if by magic, the requested Uncle showed up in the doorway to the kitchen. He looked around and asked, "Did I hear a pretty young lady asking for me?"

"Me, Me!" Hannah yelled and wiggled out of her mother's arms.

Running over, she jumped into Taggert's arms. Raelynn looked embarrassed because his shirt was now streaked with dirt from Hannah's hands. He didn't seem to mind, only looked over and asked, "Is it okay, Momma, if Hannah sits with us, if she promises to be a good girl?"

Hannah smiled, "I be good, Mama!" she yelled.

Raelynn nodded, and they went back into the Great Room.

"I cannot believe it," Charlotte said, "she is usually so reserved around people."

Lily nodded and added, "Yeah, I had to practically bribe that child just to let me get near her."

Shaking her head, Raelynn said, "I don't know, but she seems to love her Ucle Agger."

They all laughed again.

Later on in the afternoon, with a sleeping Hannah in his arms, Taggert decided to call his mother. The others left to give him some privacy. Raelynn offered to take Hannah off his hands but he shook his head no.

After dialing the number, he waited.

Claire picked up the phone and asked her son, "How are you?"

"Good," Taggert said quickly, "Mom, they're all very kind people; everyone has made me feel really welcome."

Sighing with relief, Claire wasn't very surprised by this. She'd met Rachael Rhodes just after Taggert was born and was impressed then, with how gracious the woman had been. It couldn't have been easy, knowing your husband faltered, and had a child be the outcome of it. And yet, she welcomed the child into her home and family.

She realized her son was waiting for her to speak, "I'm so glad, honey."

Taggert knew this wasn't easy for his mother either. "Miss Rachael extended an invitation to you to join us tomorrow if you'd like to."

This was something that Claire didn't expect. "I, uh, I'd like to be there, at least for you."

Nodding, Taggert answered, "Then please come, Mom."

They spoke for a few more minutes. Taggert gave her the hotel information and let her know he'd make sure there was a room for her there.

After ending the call, Taggert sat on the sofa, rocking a, still sleeping, Hannah. He whispered, "Oh little one, how nice it is to just sleep so peacefully."

"It is, isn't it," a voice said from across the room.

Raelynn came in to let him know they were all having coffee in the kitchen and watched him hold her daughter, as if he'd been holding her since she was born. There was a great capacity to love inside of Taggert, but Raelynn would bet that most people didn't see that side of him.

She walked closer, "I'm sorry if I startled you," Raelynn whispered as she sat down across from him. "I can take her from you. I promise she won't wake up, she sleeps like a log."

Taggert absently rubbed his cheek against Hannah's soft curls, "I actually enjoy it," he flushed, "but not in some creepy way."

Chuckling, Raelynn offered, "I know what you meant; you're fine. I find myself so comforted just by having her in my arms."

Nodding, Taggert asked, "Seth said you have another daughter, Hailey?"

Raelynn beamed, "Yes, she'll be in tomorrow morning. She's away at school on the East Coast. She's getting her Master's Degree in Education."

"You must be proud," Taggert said.

Seth came in and sat down beside his wife, "We are very proud of her."

It was easy for Taggert to see that; he may not have been Hailey's father from birth, but he was her Daddy now and he fiercely loved her.

"You know," Seth said to Raelynn, "it's going to take an act of war to extricate her from Taggert when she wakes up."

Nodding, Raelynn sighed, "I know."

Smiling, Taggert appreciated the interplay between the couple. Ever since he set foot on this property, he was shown nothing but acceptance and warmth. There was love here, love of family for sure, but a general kind of niceness that he found the rest of the world lacked most days.

Lily stood beside the sofa, observing the new "brother." She listened to his conversation with Raelynn and Seth, not wanting to intrude. He intrigued her. She could see he was thinking about something so she asked him, "What were you just thinking about?"

Having not seen Lily Fontaine enter the room, Taggert was surprised. He guessed that maybe he should amend his earlier thought; everyone made him feel welcomed and accepted….except for her.

Not one to lie or put on airs, Taggert looked at her and answered, "I was thinking that this family is nicer than most people."

She didn't believe for one moment that his words were the entire truth, but she knew he wasn't lying. Nodding, she sat down on the same sofa he was seated, but made sure there was enough room between them to be appropriate.

"I'm jealous," she confessed, "that child wouldn't go near me for months." She looked over to Raelynn, who nodded in confirmation, "and in like what, ten minutes, you come waltzing in here and she's putty in your hands."

Seth was trying not to laugh as he squeezed his wife's hand.

Taggert looked at her, blank faced, and responded, "Well, I guess you just don't have a way with women."

Raelynn bit her lip to keep from laughing but Seth busted out.

Ken Jr. and Charlotte came in to see what was so funny and smiled when they saw Seth doubled over.

Lily pursed her lips in exasperation. "It's easy to win over a three year old, Mr. Rhodes. I'm not so sure you'd do as well with a thirty year old woman."

"Ooooohhhh," Ken Jr., crooned, and received a poke in the side from his wife, who was also smiling.

Sitting forward, Seth announced, "I think the gauntlet was just thrown down, Taggert."

His eyes not leaving Lily's, Taggert answered his brother with, "I think you may be right, Seth."

Chapter 4

That evening, sitting in the kitchen, Lily was getting ready to leave. Taggert left just after dinner, letting them know that his mother would, indeed, be attending the funeral the next day.

Soon after, Ken Jr. and Charlotte took their kids back to the guest house they were staying in, to settle down for the night. Seth offered to do Hannah duties so Raelynn could visit with Lily and Rachael a while longer. They sat in the kitchen, coffee cups in hand, and talked about a lot of different things.

"Lily Fontaine," Rachael said, getting up from the table, "I have known you since the day you were born and I know when you've got something on your mind." She walked over to a cupboard and pulled out a bottle of liquor.

Raelynn smiled, "Okay, now we're talking," and got up herself to grab some glasses.

Lily didn't have any place to be just then so she figured a quick drink wouldn't hurt. "Fine," she almost whined. "I just can't shake the feeling of betrayal here."

Nodding, Rachael poured a generous amount of liquor into the glasses and handed them to the other women. "Betrayal about what?" she asked Lily.

They clinked their glasses and each downed the drink.

'Whiskey,' Lily thought to herself. Appropriate.

Feeling the heat of the liquor, Lily let it sink in for a minute before answering. "He didn't tell his sons that they have a brother!" She said it louder than intended, and felt bad.

Patting Lily's hand, Rachael nodded, "You can say that, but I'd like to think that he had some reason that none of us understood, but, when it really counted, he acknowledged Taggert."

Raelynn nodded in agreement, "As far as I can tell, Taggert was brought up very well. He's polite, well-mannered, and, let's face it, handsome."

All three of them laughed.

"I'm sorry, Mrs. Rhodes," Lily murmured, "It wasn't my place to say anything."

Looking astonished, Rachael asked, "Since when?"

Frowning, Lily didn't understand what she meant.

Squeezing Lily's hand, Rachael commented, "You've been in our house, and this one more than almost anyone and you practically grew up as a surrogate sister to Seth and Ken. I think you've earned the right to speak your mind."

"Amen," Raelynn announced, and poured them each another drink.

Seth came downstairs, after putting a very tired Hannah to bed, and found his mother, his wife, and Lily sitting at the kitchen table, drinking....alcohol.

"Do my eyes deceive me?" he asked and winked at his mother.

Rachael smiled at her son, "No, you're mother, your wife, and your sister are all getting drunk." Her voice was a little shaky from the alcohol.

Laughing, Seth came over and sat beside Raelynn. "Can I join in?" he asked.

Without saying anything, Raelynn poured a good three finger amount into her glass and handed it to her husband. He downed it and sighed. "Good stuff."

Lily nodded, and turned to Seth, "So what do you think of your brother?" she asked.

Seth smiled, "I think he's good people; he reminds me a bit of Dad," he looked at his mother when he spoke.

Rachael nodded, "Yes, I suppose he does in a way."

"You guys are making it really hard for me to dislike this guy, you know that?" Lily asked as she moved her glass over for Raelynn to refill it.

Frowning, Seth asked her, "Why do you dislike him?"

She downed the drink Raelynn poured for her and squeezed her eyes shut as the liquor pooled in her belly, "Because," she answered, her speech slurring a little, "he's waltzing in here, taking part of your inheritance, and," she waited, "and," a sigh, "I don't know what else, but there was more."

"You're drunk," Rachael announced, then hiccupped before saying, "so am I."

They laughed as Seth pouring them another round.

Raelynn couldn't resist; she pointed at Lily and said, "I think he's sweet on you."

Seth laughed, and teased, "Lily and Taggert sitting in a tree...."

Then it was Rachael's turn, "I heard that there was some sort of dare about impressing women."

"Oh, oh," Seth piped up, "Yes! She basically dared him to show her how good he was."

Lily just shook her head, "That man wouldn't know how to sweep me off my feet if I handed him the broom in which to do it," she took another swig, "And anyway, he's not my type."

Raelynn almost choked while she was drinking, "Not your type?" she asked, appalled. "He's every woman's type."

"Hey!" Seth became offensive.

Touching her husband's arm, Raelynn crooned, "Of course he's not as handsome as you are, but he's not bad."

They laughed and drank some more.

Lily woke up, her head throbbing, and found herself on the couch in the Great Room, a blanket draped over her.

When she opened her eyes, she found she was being studied by a very curious three year old.

"Hello, Ms. Lillleee," Hannah said.

The way Hannah pronounced her name always made Lily laugh. Unfortunately, it really hurt to laugh right now.

Raelynn came in the room and said, "Hannah, leave Ms. Lily alone. She's not feeling too good."

Hannah patted Lily's arm, "It's ok," she tried to make her friend feel better.

Smiling, Lily sat up and accepted the cup of coffee Raelynn offered her. "Thank you," she said.

Running after the sound of her cousins, Hannah disappeared.

"Sorry about her waking you up," Raelynn said.

Waving her hand, Lily answered, "She didn't, and I need to get up and get going." After looking at her phone, she cringed, "Oh Lord, I'll get going and make it back for the funeral."

Nodding, Raelynn answered, "Okay, we'll see you then."

After going home and showering in record time, Lily got dressed and returned to the Rhodes Ranch. She liked that name a lot better than SS Ranch that Seth used to have.

He renamed it that when he took over from his dad, using his initials and his fiancé's, at the time. Thank the Lord he got out of that relationship. That crazed out psychopath tried to hurt him and Raelynn after they'd gotten together.

Shaking off her sporadic thoughts, Lily knew she was a lawyer today. She would mourn with the rest of the family and friends for a while, but then it was her turn to go over the legal part of this.

There were already dozens of cars parked in the driveway by the time Lily made her way up toward the main house. Seth told her she could park on the far side of the house, where only family was parking, so she made her way slowly around the drive.

People were milling around the area, some walking over to the barn to pay their respects to the staff, or look at the horses out in the paddock.

She grabbed her briefcase and got out of her car. The first person she saw was, of course, Taggert. He did look rather handsome, Lily would admit that at least.

His dark suit was fitted to him and gave him a masculine appearance. His black cowboy hat and black cowboy boots made him look like he could be reckless or serious, depending on the situation.

Making her way over toward him, Lily nodded and merely gave him a quick grin in greeting. "Mr. Rhodes," she said, all business.

"Ms. Fontaine," Taggert drew out in his southern drawl.

As much as Hannah saying her name made her smile, the way Taggert said her name, made her "aware." There was a shot of electricity that ran along her skin as the words left his mouth.

Trying to keep her composure, Lily simply nodded again and went inside.

Once past Taggert, she felt at ease. What Rachael said last night was true; she'd been on this ranch her whole life, it was a second home to her, and she wouldn't let anyone, not even Taggert Rhodes, make her feel uncomfortable here.

"Lily," her mother said and came over to kiss her daughter's cheek.

Smiling, Lily looked at her mother, who looked exquisite, as always. Ginny Fontaine was from the old school of "always look like a lady." She had every hair in place, an appropriate black dress, and a genuine string of pearls around her neck.

Trying to keep her emotions in check, Lily whispered, "You look so pretty, Mommy."

Ginny smiled at her daughter. Whenever Lily used the term "mommy," it meant she was having a tough time. Not that Ginny disliked it, she actually was relieved that her daughter still needed her sometimes.

"Thank you, sweetheart," Ginny whispered back, "Let's go inside and see Rachael and the boys."

They walked into the Great Room and Lily was astonished by the change in the few hours since she'd woken up on the sofa.

All the furniture had been moved out of the room with folding chairs lined up in their places. At the front of the room, next to the giant fireplace, was Ken Sr.

Family members and friends were standing, or sitting, but everyone was talking about Ken Sr. It was a laugh here, or a tear there, but it was all about how much this man was loved.

Leaving her mother's side, Lily went up to where the casket was displayed.

Ken Sr. looked peaceful, a cowboy hat in his hands. Lily looked at him, noticing the rose on his lapel, no doubt a suggestion from Rachael. There were pictures lining the back of the casket and Lily took a few moments to look at them. Most were of Rachael and the boys, but there were a few more.

One in particular caught her eye. It was of a little boy, standing next to a horse.

"I didn't know he had it," Taggert said from behind her.

Lily turned around and Taggert pointed at the picture.

She smiled, "That's you?" she asked.

Taggert nodded, "That was the first horse I ever had. My mom never told me that he bought it." He stopped for a moment, "I thought it was a gift from her."

Feeling sorry for the loss of that poor little boy, Lily put her hand on Taggert's arm. The gesture was meant to comfort but, instead, it awoke feelings inside of her that she didn't understand. As soon as her skin touched his, her whole being jumped to attention. It was if her insides had been sleeping before, and Taggert woke her up from the inside out.

"I thought I knew him so well," Lily dropped her hand and said softly. "I didn't know him at all it seems."

Pretty sure that Lily wasn't really talking about Ken Sr., Taggert let the comment go. Everyone grieved in their own way.

When her mother came up beside her, Lily turned and looked at her, "Mom, this is Taggert Rhodes."

Surprise, quickly covered, Ginny extended her hand, "Taggert, so nice to meet you."

Nodding, Taggert took her hand, "My pleasure, ma'am."

Looking behind him, he asked, "Lily, would you care to come over to meet my mother?"

Before Lily could answer, Ginny took her arm and steered her toward the chairs, "Of course," she answered.

They followed Taggert. Lily was sure this woman was not his mother; she looked too young to have a son in his mid-thirties.

"Mom," Taggert said, "this is Lily Fontaine, the lawyer for Ken's estate, and her mother..."

Ginny extended her hand and offered, "Ginny Fontaine."

Claire was feeling mostly like an interloper so it was nice to see some kind faces. "Nice to meet you. I'm Claire Walden."

Sitting down next to Claire, Ginny took the woman's hand into her own, "So tell me all about Taggert when he was a little boy."

Lily was confused as to why her mother was making fast friends with Taggert's mother. Not that she couldn't, or shouldn't, it was just odd since Ginny was such good friends with Rachael.

"Thinking again?" Taggert whispered into her ear.

He was close, too close, and his breath on her ear made her skin tingle. She stepped away, more for self-preservation, than anything else.

Spotting Raelynn and Seth, Lily made her way toward them, without a word to Taggert. It was rude, but she wasn't here to be seduced by some cowboy; she was here to say goodbye to a friend and do her job.

Waiting for Raelynn to finish speaking with another guest, Lily stood there, glancing around, mostly to make sure that Taggert Rhodes stayed on the other side of the room.

"Lily," Raelynn said, "you look scared."

Shaken out of her thoughts, Lily smiled, "No, not at all. Sorry."

Taking Lily's arm, Raelynn steered her toward the den, "Seth is in here with Rachael."

Nodding, Lily blindly followed Raelynn, hoping she would be able to get a breath into her lungs. It seemed that Taggert Rhodes thought it was his mission to steal it from them in the first place.

They went into the den and saw Rachael sitting down on a settee, with Seth beside her.

He looked relieved to see his wife and Lily. "It seems Mom is having a difficult time," he said and stood so Raelynn could take his place.

Frowning at her son, Rachael countered, "I'm not having a difficult time, Seth, so don't patronize me. I just don't want to say goodbye to your father yet."

"Seems perfectly reasonable to me," Lily retorted, and smiled at the nasty, brotherly look Seth shot her.

Raelynn sat down and said, "Seth, could you go out and get your mom a glass of ice water, please?"

He nodded and practically ran from the room.

Rachael shook her head in exasperation, "Men!" she shot out, and then giggled at her own outburst.

Raelynn laughed, "Amen, again!"

Lily was so grateful to know these women. "Rachael, we'll wait as long as you want."

Looking down at her watch, Rachael sighed, "No, Ken hated it when I was late when he was alive, and I won't disappoint him now, during our last time together."

Lily had to look away, the tears filled her eyes quickly. The words spoke of love that didn't know the mere boundaries of life.

After checking her face in a little compact mirror, Rachael shrugged and motioned for them to get going.

Ken Jr. came in and, noticing that his mother was coming out, started to gather the guests in the Great Room.

People were sitting down in the rows of chairs that were set up. There was a little murmuring as guests greeted one another or asked if seats were taken. Within minutes though, every seat was filled, with dozens of people standing.

Rachael sat in the front row, her sons flanking her, and their wives beside them. Taggert was about to sit down next to his mother when Seth said, "Taggert, we'd like you to sit up here with us."

Looking at his mother, tears in her eyes and nodding, Taggert turned and sat down in the front row, next to Raelynn.

Lily sat in the chair right behind him, right between his mother and hers.

The service began, the pastor of the local church standing up. "Thank you all for coming today. As you know, Ken Rhodes Sr. didn't care for a bunch of fuss, so he probably wouldn't appreciate so many people coming out to say goodbye." There were some chuckles and heads nodding. "But, I know his family appreciates it. Rachael, his wife, his sons, Ken Jr., Seth, and Taggert," there were murmurs.

Lily looked around and saw a lot of confused faces. The family and close friends were told about Taggert a few days ago, but the rest of the town obviously didn't know. She listened to the Pastor as he read Ken's favorite passage from the Bible. There was a song played, then Ken Jr. stood up and gave the eulogy for his father.

When it was all said and done, the service was beautiful and everyone was asked to start making their way to the family cemetery, which was a short walk from the house. The family planned to stay and say one last goodbye before the casket was closed.

Lily was about to stand, when her mother's hand clamped onto her arm, silently asking her to stay. She sat back down and watched as the boys said goodbye to their dad.

Chapter 5

Taggert walked up to the casket, and looked down at his father. This was the first, and last, time he would see his father's face. Feeling a profound sense of loss, he started breathing heavy; there was no way to describe the helplessness he felt.

Lily could see Taggert struggling to keep his emotions in check. She looked at her mother, who nodded, then got up to go over to him.

"I know," she said and put her arm around his side.

He looked down at Lily, tears in his eyes, and asked, "Why?"

She couldn't answer, only allowed him to lean on her as they walked out of the room.

Rachael waited, as the boys said their goodbyes, and left to walk over to the cemetery. She turned around and nodded to Ginny before turning her eyes to Claire Walden. "I thought," she said, her voice catching, "that you might want to say a private goodbye."

Crying openly, Claire Walden smiled at Ken's wife. "We said our goodbyes a long time ago, Rachael, but thank you for the opportunity." She reached forward and patted Rachael's hand, "I'm sorry for your loss." She stood and walked out of the room.

"This is it," Ginny Fontaine said to her friend.

They stood together, then, arm in arm, walked over to the casket.

"Well, he looks good," Ginny commented, and gained a laugh from Rachael.

Reaching down, to stroke her husband's cheek one last time, Rachael said, "He always did," and shook with sadness.

Holding her friend, Ginny spoke, "I look particularly good today, and if you make me cry, remember I don't look good when I'm crying…"

Her friend's words were the only thing keeping Rachael from collapsing into a ball on the floor. "No, you don't," she said and looked at her friend. "You'll have to help me, Gin," she whispered, the tears choking off her words.

Smiling, Ginny returned, "I'll help you."

The two women left the room, hearing the casket being closed.

Minutes later, the crowd gathered around the gravesite in the family cemetery. The ranch hands volunteered to be the pallbearers so that the boys could stay with their mother. Rachael thought that was very appropriate since Ken Sr. always had a good rapport with the men who worked on the ranch.

She, again, stood between her sons as the pastor said a few more words and quoted a Bible verse.

Rachael took a red rose from one of the dozens of arrangements and walked over to the casket. She lay the rose on the casket, and leaned forward to kiss it. "Goodbye, my love," she whispered one last time.

Taggert watched Rachael and knew that she loved her husband. Looking over, he watched his own mother, to see how she was holding up. Any love Claire felt for Ken Sr., if she did love him at all, ended years earlier.

That was the best legacy to leave, to Taggert anyway, one that included love.

After the service, there was a buffet set up in the backyard under a large tent. Mrs. Bentler was dabbing her cheeks with a tissue in between issuing orders for the catering staff.

Lily stayed with her mother and Rachael, for most of the time, making sure they were okay. She also kept an eye on Taggert. Now that the whole town knew he was Ken Sr.'s son, there were bound to be questions and comments.

She also noticed quite a few young ladies hanging around him, offering something that wasn't quite what she would describe as condolences.

"Will you please excuse me?" Lily asked her mother, before making her way through the crowd.

She managed, quite quickly, to get through his "ladies in waiting," such as they were and gave him a look of disapproval. "Are you having fun?" she asked, the sarcasm dripping off of her words like warm molasses.

Looking over, Taggert was fit to be tied. He didn't have one damn thing to do about all this female attention. And he sure as hell didn't need this know-it-all lawyer making him feel bad about it.

"Ladies," he announced, "If you'll excuse me, Miss Fontaine and I have some personal business to attend to."

The ladies took it poorly and Lily couldn't help but notice the multitude of nasty looks shot in her direction. Rolling her eyes, she almost yelped when she felt Taggert's hand wrap around her arm and half drag her toward the house.

Raelynn was standing near the edge of the tent, on the side closest to the house, when she saw Taggert and Lily heading to the side door. Intrigued, she gently nudged her husband's side to get his attention, and nodded toward the couple when he looked at her questioningly.

"I'll be," Seth whispered, a smile forming for the first time today.

Not sure she was as okay with, what appeared to be, Taggert and Lily trying to find some privacy, Raelynn noted the time and would give them fifteen minutes.

"What are you doing?" Lily hissed through gritted teeth as Taggert pulled her inside the house.

He didn't answer; couldn't answer just then. Everything was too tumultuous inside his chest. All the feelings of anger, resentment, regret, and, he assumed, fondness for his new family were raging around like a dust storm inside of him.

Once he found the study was empty, he pulled her in with him and shut the door.

He released her as quickly as he grabbed her, causing Lily to absently rub her arm where his fingers touched her. She was boiling mad. "Taggert Rhodes," she huffed, "you cannot just manhandle me like that!"

He stood across the room, his hands on the fireplace hearth in front of him, his head bend down, and his shoulders so tight, he thought they might snap from the tension running through them. He still didn't answer.

Lily stomped over to where he stood and jammed her hands on her hips in exasperation. "Taggert!" Her voice even louder now. She was going to say more but she caught the look on his face, just a quick glance, before he turned away but she still saw it…turmoil and pain.

She didn't know what to do; Lily never was the comforting type and she didn't even know this man. But, for some reason, she searched her own heart, and reached out to gently place her hand on Taggert's shoulder.

Taggert was trying to keep her from seeing him like this; he hated being vulnerable, and yet, this Lily Fontaine, she saw it. As soon as she put her hand on his shoulder, some of that pain eased. Even that confused him. She was a virtual stranger, and yet her touch soothed him. This was all too much; he couldn't understand it.

Standing there, next to Taggert, her hand gently rubbing his shoulder, Lily sensed something in the room. A heaviness, maybe a little fear, but as strange as it all seemed, there was also something that seemed so right about it too.

Pushing away from where he was standing, he shifted to face her. Unshed tears in the back of his eyes, the pain of hiding all of this was too much, so he let go. He leaned forward, pulling Lily to him. One arm was wrapped around her waist, the other was cupping her neck so he could feel her pulse as it beat quickly against his touch.

Looking up at Taggert, Lily knew what his intentions were. It was wrong, she knew it, but she couldn't stop herself from leaning toward him, silently inviting him to kiss her.

If Taggert thought, for even a second, that kissing Lily would only make his insides spin more, he wouldn't have done it. Her lips matched his in every way. She opened to him and met his eagerness with her own, her tongue flicking against his in a purely sexual way.

His lips were everywhere at once, in Lily's mind. Lily knew, logically, that this was just a manifestation of his grief, but it felt so good she couldn't stop.

Taggert couldn't move his hands; if he did, he knew he'd pull her clothes off right now and bury himself in her. That wasn't something a gentleman did. He, very slowly, pulled his head away, opening his eyes as he did.

Lily was looking up, her eyes lifting open, and the fog of need clearing. The pain was still there, in Taggert's eyes, but she saw the need there too, she knew it, probably because it matched her own.

"Excuse me," a voice came from the doorway.

Startled, Lily jumped away from Taggert and absently straightened her clothing. She saw Raelynn, standing there, looking worried.

Stepping forward, Taggert spoke first, clearly embarrassed. "I'm sorry, Raelynn. I realize that this isn't appropriate but Lily was kind enough to come inside and I was having difficulty dealing with all of this."

Putting her hands up, Raelynn smiled, "Taggert," she said softly, "I am not here to reprimand you, or Lily. I'm just checking on you to make sure you're okay." She looked over at a blushing Lily. "I can see that you are, so, I'll leave you be."

As the door closed, Lily's shame came over her like a cloud. "Oh my Lord," she said. "What am I doing?"

Taggert was going to say something when she walked out of the room, closing the door behind her. He stood there for a few minutes, then sat down in the sofa and looked at nothing.

Rachael came up to Seth, and asked, "Have you seen Taggert and Lily?"

He shrugged and was about to relay what he saw earlier with Raelynn, when she came around the side of the house.

Seeing her mother-in-law, Raelynn blew out a calming breath and smiled. She would be strong for Rachael today, no matter what. Going into the study and seeing Lily with Taggert was a little much to take in, but she'd deal with it.

Smiling at Raelynn, Rachael asked her, "Have you seen Lily and Taggert?"

Nodding, Raelynn stood beside her husband, before answering, "They were inside talking."

Just then, Lily came around the side of the house and made her way toward her mother.

Ginny caught Rachael's eye and motioned for her to come over, so she excused herself from Seth and Raelynn.

Looking at his wife, Seth knew something was up. "They weren't talking, were they?" he asked his wife as he wrapped his arm protectively around her waist.

Raelynn shook her head no, then added, "Remember the day at the cabin out on the ranch?" He nodded, and she raised her eyebrows until he caught on.

"They weren't'?" he asked, shocked.

Raelynn looked over to see a, still flushed, Lily speaking to Rachael and Ginny. "No, not the whole thing, just the kissing," she whispered into her husband's ear.

Seth remembered, all too well, those early days with Raelynn. The want, the need, the desire, that raged through him. He still felt all those things, even four years later; he was just used to being more open with her now. "Are you sure?" he asked.

For the first time, Raelynn smiled about the situation. "Seth Michael Rhodes, do you think I don't know what two people in a passionate embrace look like?"

Moving so he was facing her, Seth winked, "I don't know, do I need to demonstrate so you have something to compare it to?"

He was about to follow through when he felt a hand on his back. Turning around, Seth saw it was their daughter, Hailey. He picked her up into his arms and gave her a big hug, "Welcome home," he whispered into her ear.

Raelynn's eyes brightened, "Hailey," she whispered, and hugged her daughter when Seth put her down.

"Mom, Seth," Hailey said, tears in her eyes, "I'm so sorry I missed Grandpa Rhodes' funeral."

Smiling, Seth said, "It's fine, you're here now." He kissed her forehead, "Why don't you go over and see Grandma?" He pointed to where Rachael stood.

Nodding, Hailey tried to give them a brave smile before walking over to where her Grandma Rhodes was talking with Mrs. Fontaine and Lily.

Raelynn put her hands on her husband's back and leaned her chin on his shoulder, "You know, I think that's why I married you," she waited until he turned to look at her, "you love Hailey as your own."

Seth pulled his wife into his arms, tucking her head under his chin. "I have four women in my life: my wife, my momma, and my two daughters; I'm the luckiest man in the world."

A tear slid down Raelynn's cheek. There were moments during the day that she compared this day to the one when Hailey's father, Anthony, was laid to rest. Even twenty-three years later, she could remember each painful moment and she prayed that Rachael didn't have to go through that.

"How are you holding up?" Seth asked her as he absently rubbed her back.

He'd always known, from the beginning, what Raelynn was thinking or feeling. It was some magical connection between them that Raelynn was thankful for ever since. She nodded against his chest, "I'm okay," and she meant it.

Lily watched as Rachael greeted Hailey Woodsen, Raelynn's daughter from her previous marriage. Even though Hailey wasn't Seth's biological daughter, that never seemed to matter to the Rhodes family. Rachael, embraced the young woman and shed tears for the first time that Lily saw.

Taggert stood by the side of the house, watching Lily. She was looking at Rachael, as she stood holding a young woman. Ginny was smiling and talking to them and Taggert had the feeling that she was family.

His eyes drifted back to Lily and he was amazed. There was a tightness in his gut now, when his eyes found her. It was some crazy thing that he knew could break him. She was beautiful, her long, dark hair drifting softly in the light breeze. Her fingers absently brushing it from her cheek, and Taggert wished it was his fingers that brushed along her skin.

He thought about going over and speaking to her, but he didn't want a replay of the crazy scene earlier, with all the women. That was embarrassing and Taggert didn't like being the center of attention on a good day, much less on the day he was laying his father to rest.

"She's very pretty," Claire whispered to her son.

Taggert started, not having heard his mother come up beside him. "Um," he mumbled, "I'm not sure what you're talking about."

Looking at her son, a dry look on her face, Claire Walden snorted, "Taggert Maxwell Rhodes," she only used his full name when she was mad or frustrated, "do you think I was born yesterday?"

Chagrined, Taggert averted his eyes, "I'm sorry, Mom, I'm just feeling emotional."

That, Claire could understand. She hugged her son and sighed, "That's the point of death; it makes us realize how tentative it all can be."

He turned, wrapping his mother's arm around his, and walked around the front of the house. "You never told me why he didn't meet me," he said as they were out of earshot of the other guests.

Walking with her son, here, was surreal to Claire. Even though it all happened decades ago, sometimes, it felt like it was just yesterday. Meeting Ken Rhodes, having him sweep her off of her feet, and show her passion, finding out she was pregnant....and that he was married with a family. Those feelings were, thankfully, less intense than they were way back then.

"I'm going to tell you things that you may, or may not, look at me negatively about so, please," She stopped and waited for Taggert to look at her. "Just listen."

He nodded and motioned for her to sit with him on the front step.

Taking a deep breath, Claire began. "He was just so big and strong and handsome," she blushed. "It was nothing that we planned; it just happened." She looked over at her son, who was a beautiful mix of her and Ken. "And when I found out he was married, and had Rachael and the boys," she let a stray tear make its way down her cheek, "I wanted you for myself."

Taggert listened to his mother, feeling sadness for her and the feeling of being pregnant and alone.

"It was a mix of wanting to prove that I was independent and not letting him have you," Claire revealed, and felt awful for that greediness now. "I think he was kind of relieved that he could keep it all hush hush." She sighed again, "Back then, a man with that kind of influence and standing couldn't just tote around an illegitimate child."

Most of what his mother said, Taggert figured out long ago. He didn't harbor resentment toward his father because his mother had been there, for everything. He really only wished that he would've known the true part his father played in his life.

Looking at his mother, her face lowered in shame. Taggert kissed her cheek and said, "I don't think poorly of either of you. You both did what you had to, in order to make the most of a tense situation and to give me a good life."

Claire lifted her face and looked at her son, their son, and knew, he was a good man.

Chapter 6

It was mid-evening when the guests began to leave. The stories were told, good ones, funny ones, some sad ones, and the ones that meant the most to those who knew Ken Sr.

The family began to file into the house, sitting in the Great Room, and waiting for Lily to come in and talk about the will.

Normally, this sort of thing would be discussed a day or two later, but, with the delay of having to contact Taggert, they all really knew what was going to be read.

Lily came into the room after spending ten minutes in the bathroom freshening up. She tried desperately to minimize the flush in her cheeks. And, trying to forget the reason her cheeks were red in the first place.

"Okay, can everyone have a seat, so we can begin?" she asked and picked up her briefcase to get out the copy of the will.

Rachael sat in an oversized chair to Lily's right. Normally she would sit with her boys, but she wanted them to be near their families for this.

Seth, Raelynn, and Hailey sat on one sofa. Hailey motioned for Taggert to sit next to her. "Hi, I'm Hailey," she said as he sat down.

Smiling, Taggert held out his hand, "I'm Taggert, your uncle."

Chuckling, Hailey nodded. "Don't feel bad about being the newbie in this family; it doesn't last long."

Nodding, Taggert whispered, "I kind of got that feeling myself the last couple of days."

Seeing that Lily was waiting for them to get settled, she sat back and waited.

Ken Jr., his wife Charlotte, and their two kids, Tyler and Becky sat on the other sofa. Mrs. Bentler stood next to them, unsure why Lily had asked her to be here for this.

"Okay," Lily said when she noticed everyone was here. "We'll begin with a quick note from Ken Sr." She picked up a letter hand written on his personal stationary.

My Dearest Family,

This is not a sad occasion, it's just one of change for you, and for me as well. I do not take it lightly, as I know how crushed I would be if I lost any of you. But, I have lived my life the best way I knew how. There are regrets, one in particular I wish to make amends for, but other than that, I felt loved and cherished by my beautiful Rachael, and loved by my boys.

All My Love to You!

There were some sniffles in the room, followed by Mrs. Bentler's comment, "He was always such a sweet talker."

The comment made Rachael smile. Her husband was definitely that.

"Now," Lily announced, as she handed the note to Rachael, "I'd like to go over the will in the parts that directly affect you. Everyone will get a copy of the paperwork. If you have any questions, no matter how uncomfortable you may feel about speaking up, please do."

Everyone looked at one another and nodded.

Seeing that everyone was okay, Lily started. "To begin, I'll read the part that has to do with the grandchildren. "I, have set up trust funds for my grandchildren, Hannah Rhodes, Tyler Rhodes, Becky Rhodes, Amy Rhodes, Ken Rhodes III, and Hailey Woodsen.""

Hailey's head shot up, shock covering her features. She looked at her mother and Seth, who just smiled.

Lily started again, "My beautiful wife, Rachael, and I have discussed what she felt she needed for herself, and she will be residing in our current home and have a yearly income based on investments and a separate account for her use only."

Looking down at Rachael, Lily waited for her nod to go ahead before continuing. "To my children, any debt you may have for your properties, will be paid off in full."

Ken Jr. looked at Seth, questions in his eyes. "I don't understand."

Rachael leaned forward, and spoke up, "When you bought your ranch up in Wyoming and Seth purchased this ranch from us, your father bought out the mortgages." She smiled at her oldest son, "He wanted to make this easy for the both of you."

Ken Jr. nodded at his mother, and took his wife's hand. Seth looked down, smiling. "He was really sneaky," he said to Raelynn, gaining a few chuckles from the others.

Lily waited for them to quiet and then spoke again. "To Mrs. Bentler, the right hand of mine, Rachael's, and now Seth's and Raelynn's, we could not have run this ranch without you. I would like you to take a long deserved vacation anywhere you want." Smiling at the look of surprise on Mrs. Bentler's face, Lily knew this next part would blow her mind. "And, I am leaving you an IRA with $500,000 dollars in it."

Seth stood up and helped Mrs. Bentler sit down. She was fanning her face and crying.

Taggert watched the events and realized that Ken Sr. was a generous man. Especially to those he loved.

"Finally," Lily said, once Seth sat back down, "to my sons. You have allowed me to be proud in ways I never would have imagined. All three of you will never know the depth of my love for you; know that I support you in all of your endeavors. The three of you will split up the main part of my estate."

Catching Lily's eye, Ken Jr. asked, "What is the main part of his estate?"

Clearing her throat, Lily explained. "At the time his will was created, the amount was about 3.5 million dollars."

All eyes looked at Lily, the silence deafening. Apparently, none of the kids knew how much money Ken Rhodes Sr. had acquired in his lifetime.

Sorting through some papers, Lily pulled one out, and said, "The main part of the estate, today, is listed as 5.8 million dollars."

The room was so silent, you could have heard a pin drop.

"How is that possible?" Seth asked.

Lily looked at Rachael and allowed her to answer.

Rachael stood up, "Your father was very careful with his money, boys. He was set on making sure you were all left with something, and your children too."

Looking at her husband, Raelynn was speechless, and saw that Seth looked just as blindsided. Her father-in-law was a very generous man.

"Oh yes," Lily added, "Should Taggert have any heirs, or Seth and Ken Jr. have additional children, there is an account that will be divided up between them."

As if it couldn't get any more fantastic, that did it. Taggert was silent, sitting on the sofa. His father, who he'd never met, just left him a huge sum of money, and provided something for his future children.

Hailey touched Taggert's hand and asked, "Are you okay?"

He shrugged, but answered, "I guess so; just really confused."

"There are a few more gifts, one to John, for being here so long, and some small gifts for some of the ranch hands who really helped throughout the years, but I am instructed to just send those gifts out separately," Lily added, before placing her paperwork back into her briefcase.

Everyone stood, whispering, not sure what they should say.

Mrs. Bentler stood up and announced, "We'll go into the dining room and have a bite to eat now."

The kids moved first, since they were always hungry. Melissa and John, Seth and Raelynn's friends, had Hannah for the evening so that she wouldn't disrupt the reading of the will.

"I can't believe he was so generous to me," Hailey said to Seth.

Hugging her to his side, Seth whispered, "You were his oldest granddaughter and he was proud of you."

Crying, she hugged him back, "I was proud to be his granddaughter too."

Raelynn could hear them and shed a tear. She looked at Taggert, who was still sitting, and walked over to him. "Are you okay?" she asked.

Not used to the concern, Taggert looked up, uncomfortable.

She sat down beside him, "It's okay to be happy, you know."

That comment had his head shooting up, his eyes colliding with Raelynn's. "I'm not sure what I feel."

"That's okay too," Raelynn stood. "There's no rule book on grief, or surprise, so you just take your time."

Lily was speaking to Rachael, who had a quick question, before she was finished getting her papers filed into her briefcase. When she did get them done, she turned around and noticed Taggert was the only one still in the room.

Torn between, wanting to sneak out without speaking to him, and concern about if he was okay, she simply stood there, briefcase in hand.

The information he was trying to process was getting all clogged up in Taggert's mind. None of this made sense to him. He fisted his hand and slammed it down on the arm of the sofa.

Seeing his emotions, Lily couldn't just walk away. Putting down her briefcase on the chair that Rachael vacated, she walked over and stood in front of him. He hadn't noticed her, lost in his own thoughts still. "Why did you kiss me?" she asked.

The question dragged Taggert into the present. He looked up into those beautiful blue eyes of Lily's, and studied them. She stood there, her hands on her hips, daring him to answer.

Standing up, he was now able to look down into those eyes, and he noticed they sparkled with mischief. "Because it felt right."

His answer was not what Lily expected. Of course, up until this moment, Taggert Rhodes had continually surprised her, so this was no different. 'Felt right?' She asked herself.

Lifting his hand up, so it cupped her cheek, he ran his thumb over her flushed skin. His hands were rough from working on a ranch, so her skin was like a soft cloud. "You feel right," he whispered to her.

The only place he was touching her was her cheek, and yet, Lily felt as though he was touching her everywhere. His eyes peeled away her, usually, tough exterior and made her feel exposed in a purely emotional way.

"Taggert," Mrs. Bentler called as she walked into the great room. Once she saw Taggert and Lily, she stopped, mumbled, "I'm sorry," and left again.

Now Lily felt as if her cheek would burn his palm, it was so hot. She supposed some of it was embarrassment, but mostly it was just because of whatever crazy thing was going on between them threatened to incinerate them at any moment.

Finally gaining strength, Lily stepped away. "If you'll excuse me," she said in a shaky breath, "I have some business to attend to."

Taggert stood there, where he was, until he heard the front door close.

After dinner, Seth asked Taggert to take a walk with him. Having always been the baby of the family, Seth felt a little out of place in the role of "big brother." He heard Mrs. Bentler talking to his mother about walking in on Taggert and Lily being "close." That, and the information from Raelynn about the kissing earlier, did concern him a little.

They walked across the drive and over to the corral. The sun was beginning to set so the men were getting the horses inside for the night. A few of the ponies were out, rambling around, as young horses did. Mamas stood with their babies, watching over them protectively.

Leaning on the corral fence, Seth looked out over the land that went on for miles past the corral. His land, his and Raelynn's home, a source of great pride for him.

"I've been talking to Raelynn," Seth started, "and we think you should be here, at the house, with us."

Taggert was a little confused, "I'm not sure what you mean," he answered, mimicking his brother's stance against the fence.

Seth didn't look at his brother, only stood there, staring ahead. "I mean that you don't need to be staying at a hotel. You need to be here with your family."

Family, Taggert rolled the word over in his head. Honestly, he hadn't given much thought to what he would do after the funeral. He never imagined his father would leave him such a large sum of money and he wanted to understand more about his brothers, and his father.

"You didn't know what you were going to do, did you?" Seth asked, finally looking over at his brother.

Shaking his head, Taggert responded, "No, not really."

Knowing he was stepping into territory that wasn't comfortable for him whatsoever, Seth added, "And I've been told that you've taken a liking to Lily."

There was something about Seth's tone that warned Taggert to tread lightly. "I, uh,….we, uh…."

Sighing, Seth tried to save him, "I'm practically a stranger to you, I realize that. But," he added emphatically, "I am your big brother and Lily is like a little sister to both Ken and I."

Boundaries were being set, Taggert realized, and he certainly didn't want to upset the tentative ties he had with his brothers. "Seth, I was raised by a good woman and was taught to be a gentleman."

Seth nodded. There really was no need to say anything else. "So it's settled then; you'll come and stay here?" he asked Taggert.

Extending his hand, Taggert waited for his brother to shake it, before answering, "Yes, sir."

After he shook his brother's hand, Seth clapped him on the shoulder, "Now, let's go inside and see if there's any more of that homemade apple pie."

Turning from the fence, Taggert replied, "I would definitely be up for that."

Rachael stood on the porch, watching her son and Taggert talk by the corral. Smiling, she looked up and whispered, "You would be proud, my love," before turning to go back inside.

Chapter 7

Lily woke up, feeling out of sorts. She slept in fits, tossing and turning, and she couldn't figure out why.

After she returned from the Rhodes Ranch, she stopped by her office to file some paperwork, then went straight home.

When she moved back to Alvin, Texas, to take over her father's law practice, she managed to buy the cutest little house near downtown.

The block was full of large, older homes, with loads of charm, but that wasn't what Lily wanted. She wanted something quaint, something she could decorate and not spend the majority of her time cleaning.

Her realtor friend found her this house, on a decent sized lot, complete with a white picket fence around it. The outside was a pale blue, complimented with white trim and shutters. Technically, it was a bungalow, but, to Lily, it was her refuge.

The living room was the focal point, done in a pale sand color and accented with bright shades of corals and blues. It was as if you walked onto a beach and, more than a few of her house guests commented on how calming the room was.

When she purchased the house, it was a bunch of little rooms, so she had a contractor take out whatever walls weren't load-bearing to open it up. The dining room now flowed into the kitchen, with a tall bar dividing them. It was small, but great for entertaining. Usually, Lily would get her cup of coffee and sit at the bar, enjoying the coziness of her little place.

This morning, however, she was still in bed, staring at the ceiling of her bedroom, and wondering why her mind kept drifting to a certain cowboy...

Making herself get out of bed, she frowned as she went into her adjoining bath room. He had NO business occupying her thoughts! None at all!

She showered, and dressed in her "lawyer clothes," a dark skirt, light blouse, and blazer. As she was putting on her makeup, she wondered, out of the blue, if Taggert would like it. "Darn it!" she yelled at her reflection in the mirror.

On her way to the office, Lily cranked up the radio. The sound of country music filled the car, making her smile. It also made her think of Taggert Rhodes, on his horse, looking all.....cowboyish. A frown replaced the smile and she pulled into the parking lot of her law practice a little too fast.

Her brakes squealed as she came to a stop and Lily prayed no one saw it.

Practically stomping into the office, Lily tried to shake off the frustration she felt by her own thoughts.

Jennifer, her assistant, smiled as she entered. "Good morning," she almost sang.

Lily's face fell. How could someone be so chipper when Lily felt so lousy? "Morning," she mumbled to Jennifer and went straight into her office.

After putting her briefcase in its assigned spot, she sat down at her desk and went over her phone messages. Nothing seemed too pressing, which was a relief.

Small town lawyers held a feast or famine type of business most of the time. It was steady enough, thanks to her father's contacts, to keep her in the black, but there were times when it seemed things were a little too quiet.

Jennifer popped her head into the office and smiled, "Don't forget your lunch date with the Fab 5 today," she said and left with a wink.

Smiling for the first time, Lily sat back in her chair. Lunch with the Fab 5 was just what she needed.

When she first moved back to Alvin, she reconnected with a friend from high school named Cathy. Being involved with her kids' education, Cathy regularly volunteered at her son's school. Through that connection, Lily was introduced to Anna, Kristin, and Nonie, also parents of kids who attended the same school.

The five of them really hit it off. Each of them was a little different; Lily having no kids, Cathy having three, Nonie having two, Kristin having four, and Anna having one. None of them were the same age, none of them did the same kind of job, but they all had such a good time when they were together that the nickname Fab 5 was created.

During their lunches, or breakfasts, when they could all correlate their schedules, they would discuss jobs, kids, husbands, boyfriends, or whatever else they could think of. Having those four women in her life made Lily feel like she was a better person.

Getting down to business at hand, a little legal dispute between two neighbors over a tree, fence, and property line, Lily decided to put everything else out of her mind.

When Jennifer popped her head into the office again, it was to remind her of her lunch date with the girls.

Eager to put down Mr. Simpson and his legal woes, Lily nodded and grabbed her jacket.

The girls tried to meet at one of the local restaurants. The one they chose today happened to have great barbeque. Her stomach growling, Lily realized she forgot to eat breakfast. Another side effect of thinking about a certain man a little too much.

She pulled into the parking lot at the restaurant, and smiled when she saw Nonie parking beside her.

They got out of their vehicles and hugged, Nonie greeting her with a, "Hi, sweetie."

"Hi, yourself," Lily responded, "how goes it?"

Nonie launched into a description of a class she was taking to keep her teaching certificate updated. Lily thought it was fascinating and applauded the fact that Nonie, not only taught, but was still a student in some respects. After law school, Lily herself was quite ready to be done with school.

They walked inside and saw Anna already sitting at a table.

"Hey there," Anna said, and stood to hug both of them. "KK, called," Anna used Kristin's nickname, "and said she was almost here."

Just then Cathy came in and walked over to the table. "Hello there," she said with a smile.

Lily always thought that Cathy's smile was contagious; it just lit up the room. "How are the kids?" she asked her friend.

Rolling her eyes as she sat, Cathy answered, "Rowdy boys."

That answer was all Lily needed. It was hard for her to see Cathy's boys being rowdy because they always seemed so quiet, but the stories their mother told, showed a whole different side to them.

Kristin joined them with a, "Sorry I'm late," to which everyone just smiled.

With such varying schedules and lives, it was a wonder the five of them could meet, much less at the same time. If someone was late, or couldn't come, there was no harm, no foul.

Anna talked about her husband's business, how it was doing really well, but kept her busy. Kristin taught gymnastics and regaled them with cute stories of little girls trying to learn how to flip. Nonie updated them on her kids as well.

Finally, all eyes turned to Lily, expectantly. She knew they wanted to know what was going on, but she didn't really want to tell them anything.

Kristin eyed her closely, "Something's up, I can see it."

The others nodded and stared at her, their gaze piercing.

"I'm fine, just busy," Lily finally replied, playing with the napkin on her lap.

Leaning in and speaking as if Lily wasn't sitting next to her, Anna started, "I heard she has a very cute looking cowboy on the hook."

There were oooohhhhs from her friends and Lily blushed. "He's not my cowboy, and I don't have him on a hook or anything else, for that matter," Lily retorted.

Nonie shook her head, "Hmm, I think she's a little to vehement about this cowboy; maybe we should google him or something."

'Oh Lord,' Lily thought to herself. This lunch was supposed to take her mind off of Taggert, not put him front and center.

Kristin nodded excitedly, "What's his name?" she asked as she pulled out her smart phone.

Cathy laughed, "His name is Taggert Rhodes, long lost brother of Seth and Ken."

It was if a hush fell over the table. Nobody said anything for a full minute. Lily glared at Cathy, wondering where she got her information.

As if reading Lily's mind, Cathy offered, "My mom's cousin, Rita, works with Mrs. Bentler on quilts for the senior citizen center and they were talking."

As far as Lily was concerned, Mrs. Bentler was a traitor, in the first degree.

"What happened?" Kristin asked.

Cathy was about to answer with whatever bit of gossip she'd received when Lily put up her hand to stop her. "I will tell you all, if you'll promise not to be sassy."

Shaking her head, Anna answered, "We cannot make such a promise, but go ahead."

Smiling, because she couldn't help herself, Lily knew these women would never judge her, so she started with, "He's Ken Sr.'s son from another relationship and hadn't met his father or brothers before now." She couldn't give away anything that was given to her legally, so she stuck with the facts that were probably already rotating around gossip tables in town. "He's lived in west Texas up until now, but I'm not sure what he'll do now."

Cathy was shaking her head, "That's not what we meant, Lily." She winked, "we want to know what YOU were doing with him."

Anna, Kristin, and Nonie all nodded greedily.

"Fine," Lily said, glaring, "we kissed because I was trying to comfort him."

Looking at her friends' faces, Lily realized she'd picked a poor choice of words.

Anna leaned over, "And just how were you comforting him?" she asked, wiggling her eyebrows.

Cathy nodded, "Yes, do tell."

Sighing, Lily tried to compose her thoughts. "He was being hit on by all these young women at the funeral for Pete's sake, so I made a comment to the effect of, 'Are you enjoying this?' and he got upset." She refolded the napkin on her lap, "We went inside, him half-dragging me really, and I realized he was really thrown by what was going on. I put my hand on his back to rub it, platonically," she emphasized, "and then, we were kissing."

Still waiting for more, none of them said anything.

Finally, Kristin asked, "And?"

Lily rolled her eyes, "And it was….pretty fabulous."

"OOOHHHH," Anna drew out, "Is he big and strong and manly?" she asked.

Cathy nodded, "From what I here, he's just a darker version of Seth."

That got them all going, comparing Seth, who was regarded as a pretty handsome guy, to other, more famous people.

Lily sat there, watching her friends, and was torn between being amused at their comments, and embarrassed that she'd been caught kissing a virtual stranger. Handsome cowboy, not withstanding, she didn't know Taggert Rhodes. What if he had a girlfriend, or worse, a wife?

When she came up to the surface from her thoughts, her friends were talking about Mrs. Bentler again, "She said that they made the cutest couple," Cathy was saying.

Rolling her eyes again, Lily couldn't believe her friends would buy into the gossip.

"I'm sure that Taggert Rhodes will be on his way back to west Texas any day now and you'll all feel pretty silly for teasing me about a kiss," she said, feeling smug.

Later that night, Lily was sitting at her mother's house for dinner when her hopes were dashed.

Ginny always had her daughter over for dinner on Mondays. It made her feel like they were still connected, and yet, gave Lily her weekends for privacy. Not that Ginny worried all that much about privacy; Alvin was a small town and the tongues wagged there as much as anyplace else.

"I heard that you were a topic of conversation," Ginny started.

Lily sighed, "Mrs. Bentler is way too open about business that happens at the Rhodes Ranch."

Ginny smiled at her daughter, before asking, "Business? Is that what you kids are calling it these days?"

Even though Lily knew her mother was teasing her, it still stung a bit. No one wanted to be "called out" by their parent. "Mom, we kissed, that was it," she answered.

Putting her hands in her lap, Ginny commented, "I spoke to Rachael today."

Knowing this was leading somewhere, Lily dutifully asked, "And what did Ms. Rachael have to say?"

Sitting back in her chair, Ginny answered, "She informed me that Seth and Raelynn have invited Taggert to stay there at the ranch."

Lily happened to be taking a drink of her wine when her mother made the statement, and almost made her choke. Years of good manners kept the wine down with her dignity somewhat intact. "Really?" was all she managed to ask.

"Aren't you the least bit curious about why he's staying here?" Ginny inquired to her daughter.

She'd never seen Lily get this nervous when speaking about a man, and frankly, it was about time a man made her daughter nervous. After losing Maxwell, Ginny felt the pain of being alone and definitely did not want that for Lily. Having never been married Lily truly didn't know what she was missing but still, Ginny wanted her daughter to, at least, fall in love.

Gathering her composure, Lily set down her wine glass, and responded, "No, actually I'm not."

Nodding, Ginny leaned forward again, "Well then, can I interest you in some dessert?"

The change in subject was welcomed, but made Lily suspicious at the same time. Trying not to borrow trouble, she merely answered, "Yes, ma'am."

Chapter 8

The next day, Lily was sitting at her desk when she heard the front door open. She couldn't see who was entering from her office, and didn't think much about it, since Jennifer greeted all clients in the waiting area.

A few minutes later, Jennifer stuck her head into Lily's office, "Uh, Ms. Fontaine, there's a Taggert Rhodes here to see you."

'Oh great!' Lily thought to herself. 'Just what I need.....not!' Standing up, she smoothed her skirt and hoped her hair didn't look like she'd had it done by wild birds.

"Taggert," she said and put her hand out to shake his.

Coming into Lily's office was a last minute decision for Taggert. He'd been out riding and she just sort of materialized in his mind. She completely took over his thoughts lately, making him think of kisses in the study, quiet time in the great room, and he wanted to figure out what this craziness was that blew up between them like a wild fire.

Here, she was different. No less mind blowing, but still, different. There was a distance he figured she needed in order to do her job. He took her extended hand, holding it much longer than he needed to. "Ms. Fontaine," he said the words slowly.

In her whole life, no one ever said her name in such a way that she felt seduced by it. He still held her hand and she liked the connection she felt between them.

91

Finally, Taggert released her hand. "I, uh," he started to say and held his cowboy hat in front of him like a child who was in trouble. "I, uh…" he said again.

Feeling sorry for him, Lily offered, "You wanted to ask me something?" It was just a guess, but he looked really nervous.

Nodding in assent, Taggert sighed. "I wanted to ask you if you'd like to accompany me out for a ride this evening?"

The question surprised Lily, "Is this in a lawyer-client context?" she countered.

Knowing she was teasing him helped Taggert calm down. He wasn't usually so clumsy around women, but his brother's warning, as well as his response to her, cautioned him to go slowly. He looked down into her eyes, "I think you and I both know I don't look at you as a lawyer, and I'm definitely not your client."

Lily stood there, her hands clasped in front of her. "Technically, it's a gray area since I'm executor of your father's estate, but I'm more interested in how you see me."

Oh, she was going to make him work for it, but he supposed he would've been disappointed if she hadn't. He took her hands into his and brought them up to his lips, taking an achingly slow time kissing her delicate knuckles.

They were standing in her office, fully clothed, but Taggert kissing her skin like this made her feel extremely exposed. She gently pulled her hands from his light grasp, blushing.

"I think you've made your point." She put her hands behind her back, lightly brushing her fingers across the back of her hand.

He stood there, hat in hand, literally, and asked, "So will you come out riding with me tonight?"

Every molecule in her body was screaming for her to say no, this was not a good idea. Her conscience yelled, 'You know what happens when you play with fire.' But, she found herself nodding and asking, "What time?"

Taggert smiled, "How about seven?" He knew he'd be done with some other things he needed to do by then.

Lily nodded, "See you then," she added.

He just smiled, and turned to go. Nodding his thanks to Jennifer, he glanced back at Lily when he opened the door, then left.

Watching him walk out to his truck, from her office doorway, Lily found she liked to just watch him. He moved very gracefully for a man.

Jennifer sighed, "Wow!"

Looking over at her assistant, Lily stayed quiet, but inside she was saying 'Wow!' herself.

With her plans now changed, Lily walked over to her desk. She had to get done early today, if it was possible to do so.

Taggert worked with Seth on the ranch. He didn't think that Seth really needed his help as much as he wanted to get to know Taggert and see what kind of man he was.

They were out checking fences when Seth chuckled.

Looking over, Taggert asked, "What's so funny?"

"I was just thinking about Raelynn." He turned so he was facing Taggert, "she came out with John to check and repair fences not long after we started dating and I freaked out."

Since Seth didn't seem like the "freaking out" type, Taggert asked him, "Why?"

Adjusting his horse, Lex's, position, so he was right beside Taggert, he said, "Basically, I was being an over-protective ass." Laughing at Taggert's raised eyebrows, he added, "There was a woman before Raelynn who was pretty much a nut case and I just assumed all women, Raelynn included, were just in a relationship to be taken care of."

Nodding, Seth knew his sister-in-law well enough, after just a few days, that she didn't need anyone to "take care" of her. "Ahhh," he replied.

"Yep," Seth said, prodding Lex to move forward toward the next section of fence, "my wife has her own mind, that's for sure."

Taggert agreed with him, but was intrigued as well. "So, if you don't mind my asking, was it tough for you and Raelynn in the beginning?"

They rode further down the fence line before Seth answered. He never thought of himself as someone who could dish out relationship advice, but, here he was, being a big brother. "Well, let's just say, we both had some pretty hefty hang ups."

Adjusting his cowboy hat, so it provided more shade from the late afternoon sun, he contemplated his next question. "I was hoping it was okay with you if Lily and I went out riding tonight?"

Seth wanted to laugh, Taggert sounded like a high school boy. Instead, he just said, "Sure, I'll make sure the boys know to saddle up Blue Boy for her."

"Blue Boy?" Taggert asked.

Dismounting to tighten some fence wire, Seth nodded, "Yep, Blue Boy is her horse. He's older than dirt, for a horse, but he's hers and hers alone."

For some weird reason, Taggert felt jealous…of the horse.

Watching Taggert, Seth almost felt sorry for him. The key word being, almost. A blind man could see that Taggert was sweet on Lily. The question in Seth's mind was, 'Was Lily sweet on Taggert?' He only knew what Mrs. Bentler and Raelynn told him.

Taggert finished the ride in silence. He had a lot to think about. What he was going to do here, what he was going to do about the job waiting for him back in West Texas, and what the hell he was going to do about the gorgeous lawyer?

Earlier that morning, he said goodbye to his mother. She was going back to her job and life and had absolutely no qualms about him staying here. He was kind of surprised, honestly, he thought maybe she would be a little leery of his "family" here but she was all for it.

He kissed her cheek and waved as she drove off. They were close all of his life and he never doubted, no matter where he lived, that they would be until the end.

Now, he just needed to figure out his life.

Lily left work, in a hurry, of course. A meeting with Mrs. Mueller regarding contributions to the city's historical society, in the event of her death, took longer than she planned. Mrs. Mueller was a woman of sixty, who was probably the healthiest of anyone her age in the area, but who was afraid she would "expire" at any moment.

It was already almost six when she walked into her house.

She ate a salad quickly, not even caring that the lettuce had seen better days.

Changing into her riding gear, which consisted of well-worn jeans, a light top over a camisole, and her favorite cowboy boots, took little time. It was when she went to braid her hair that Lily had trouble. Her fingers wouldn't cooperate for some reason. "Probably because you're nervous," she grumbled as she glared into the mirror. After three tries, she got the strands to do what she wanted. She spritzed a little body mist on and left the house.

The ride out to the Rhodes Ranch was familiar, since she was basically out there weekly. She either visited with Seth and Raelynn, or just went out to ride her Blue Boy.

Smiling, Lily loved her horse. Blue Boy was a gift from her father, who won him in a poker game. They'd been together for fifteen years and she always said he was the only man, besides her daddy, she wanted to keep in her life for that period of time. He stood a little over fourteen hands, was black, and had a star shaped mark on his nose.

She turned into the driveway and slowed down, trying not to get dust all over her car.

Peeking at the mirror, she murmured, "You are so vain, Lily Fontaine." It was a little rhyme she used when she was fed up with her little eccentricities.

As she pulled the car around to the far side of the house, she saw Taggert and Seth coming out of the house.

Each time she saw them, she saw more of a resemblance between them. Even growing up far apart, some of their mannerisms were completely identical. The way they walked, the way they used their hands when they spoke, and even some of their facial reactions were eerily similar.

Seth raised her hand in greeting and walked over to open her car door. "Hello there, pretty lady," he said to Lily with a smile.

Being like a big brother to her for the better part of thirty years, Lily was comfortable with her affection for Seth. "Hey," she replied and gave him a hug.

Taggert watched his brother hug Lily and wanted to punch him in the face. 'Deal with it Rhodes,' he chastised himself.

When Lily released Seth, she turned to look at Taggert. Noticing that he didn't look very happy, she frowned.

"Evening, Ms. Lily," Taggert said, trying to shake off his crazy thoughts.

She grinned, "Evening to you, Mr. Rhodes."

He tipped his hat and said, "Please, call me Taggert."

Seth stood there and watched the two of them. It was like watching two people play chess really slowly; very frustrating for the onlookers. He shook his head and announced, "I'll just go on inside and see if Raelynn needs anything."

Neither Taggert, nor Lily, even seemed to hear him so he turned away and walked inside. Walking through the mud room, he caught his wife staring out the kitchen window. "Raelynn?" he asked, and smiled when she jumped.

"I was," Raelynn muttered, "just looking for you."

Opening his arms, he said, "I'm right here."

Trying to cover up the fact that she was snooping, Raelynn walked over and hugged her husband.

He hugged her and then pulled her with him, back over to the window. "They are being so strange," Seth said to his wife, "like they're not sure what to do."

Raelynn broke out, laughing. "Oh my Lord!" she practically yelled, "Don't you remember how it was for us?"

Turning, so he could look at his beautiful wife, Seth smiled. "I remember falling for you so hard, that I couldn't breathe."

Flattery could go a long way, in Raelynn's mind. "And I loved you so much, so fast, that I couldn't even deal with it." She looked out at Lily and Taggert, who managed to start heading for the barn. "And it took me some time. It will take them some time too."

"Time for what?" a voice asked from behind them.

Seeing her best friend and business partner, Melissa, Raelynn smiled. "Oh, we're talking about Lily and Taggert."

Melissa came over and peeked out the window, "Crud, I can't see his face."

"Just picture Seth, with a few more inches, a few less wrinkles, and dark hair," Raelynn said, being sassy.

Seth rolled his eyes, "Thanks."

Smiling, Melissa said, "Yummy."

"Hey there, aren't you a married lady?" her husband, John, said from the doorway.

Walking over to John, Melissa wrapped her arms around him and responded, "Why yes, I believe I am."

A single nod to punctuate his point, John smiled.

Seth watched his foreman, and friend, and knew that they all went through their own set of issues before they were able to get married. It would probably be the same way for Lily and Taggert.

"How's Grace?" Raelynn asked, trying to change the subject. She could see her husband was getting too serious.

Melissa sat down at the table and answered, "She's great! She and Tavin just got back from their honeymoon and she's all ga-ga!"

Grace McCormick was Melissa's niece. She'd come to Texas a few years earlier to help Melissa and Raelynn with the business. She ended up falling in love with Seth's neighbor, and friend, Tavin McCormick.

They were just married a few weeks before and were off on their honeymoon when Ken Sr. passed away. They offered to come back, but both Melissa and Raelynn insisted they stick with their original plans.

"So," Melissa asked, nodding her thanks to the coffee Raelynn just set down before her. "Are Ken Jr. and Charlotte still here with the kids?"

Seth shook his head, "No, they went back to Wyoming this morning." He handed John a cup of coffee, then sat down. "They needed to get home and get the kids back to school."

John nodded, "It was good to see both of you boys together, even under these circumstances." He tended to save his words, unless it was important.

"He was just as surprised as I was about Taggert, and the inheritance." Seth said. He felt comfortable talking family business with John, since he ran the ranch now with Seth, as their fathers together ran it before them. John was practically family.

Clearing his throat, John said, "Well, that's why we stopped by actually." He looked at Melissa, who just smiled and nodded. "Seems I got a check in the mail from Ms. Lily's law practice. You're father saw fit to give me a little money as well."

Glad, because John certainly deserved it, Seth smiled. "Great!"

"It was too much," John added, "I don't feel right taking such a gift when it should go to his kin."

Raelynn had to bite her lip to keep from crying, "John," she reached across the table and took his hand, "don't you know that you are kin?"

Uncomfortable with showing emotions, John just nodded quickly, "I suppose you're right Lynn," he used his nickname for Raelynn.

Melissa sighed, "That's what I told him, but why listen to me?" she asked sarcastically, "I'm just his wife."

They laughed.

Leaning over toward Raelynn, Melissa asked, "So tell me more about this mysterious Taggert Rhodes…"

Chapter 9

Taggert walked with Lily toward the barn and his palms were actually sweaty. It wasn't like he was a teenager who never kissed a girl, but that was exactly how he felt.

Since Lily rode here all the time, she was very familiar with the barn layout. Blue Boy's stall was empty so she figured that Taggert must have told Seth she was coming over.

They crossed through the barn and came out into the pasture side. There stood Blue Boy, saddled and ready to go. When he saw her, he nickered in recognition.

"I know," she crooned in the horse's ear, "it has been too long, I'm sorry."

Watching Lily with her horse made Taggert relax. She loved Blue Boy and had the same closeness with him that Taggert shared with Diego.

His boss laughed when he said he was taking Diego with him during his trip east for his father's funeral. With the kind of work Taggert did, his horse was important, and, having bought Diego himself, made the horse especially important. Diego was his closest friend, in a lot of respects.

He walked up behind Lily and scratched Blue Boy behind the ears.

Lily laughed, "He's usually very possessive of me and doesn't let other people near." She kept stroking the horse's neck as she spoke, "One time he nearly took Seth's hand off when he was putting on the bridle and I was next to him."

Leaning in, Taggert whispered to the horse, "I know what you mean, she's a special lady."

Standing there, watching Taggert in the fading light of daylight, whisper to Blue Boy about her being special caused her heart to race. Swallowing hard, she tried to get herself under control.

"Thank you," she said to Taggert when he finally turned from the horse and looked back at her.

He tipped her chin up with his hand, "I'll always tell you the truth, Lily," he smiled and nodded toward Blue Boy, "and him too."

She didn't doubt it for one second. And that thought scared the crap out of Lily.

"Uh," she said shakily, breaking their spell, "we should get going."

Nodding, Taggert gave her lift up into her saddle. She weighed next to nothing but seemed to sit the big horse naturally.

After he climbed up into his saddle, they started off. Taggert let Lily lead, since she was more familiar with the ranch than he was.

They walked for a while, just enjoying the sounds of the cattle in the distance, the leather of the saddles creaking, and the horses making noises here and there.

"So when did you start riding?" Taggert asked her.

Squinting, Lily thought for a second, and answered, "As far back as I can remember." She pushed her cowboy hat back a little farther so she could make eye contact with Taggert, "My dad brought me out here to Rhodes Ranch and Ken Sr. put me on a little pony."

Smiling at the thought of a little girl full of excitement, riding her first horse, Taggert smiled.

"Then I started barrel racing about sevenish, I think," Lily said while she stroked Blue Boy's nape.

Surprised, Taggert stopped and stared at her. He asked, "You were a barrel racer?"

Now Lily stopped and looked back at him, "Is that so surprising?" she asked.

'Tread lightly Rhodes,' Taggert cautioned himself. "It's not surprising that you would do it; I just figured you didn't race."

Most people had that reaction when they found out about her upbringing. It did seem a little out of context; a lawyer's daughter, at rodeos and competitions doing barrel racing. But, her father always loved the sport and sort of steered her in that direction when she showed a natural talent for it.

"When I was about fifteen, he won me Blue Boy in a poker game, and we raced for a few more years," she kissed Blue Boy's neck.

Now it was a little easier to understand her attachment to Blue Boy. In barrel racing, you HAD to be in tune with your horse if you wanted to win.

He nudged Diego back into walking, and asked, "What was your fastest time?" he asked.

"14.2 seconds," Lily answered. "On my big boy here."

That was a good time; Taggert knew it from watching his fair share of competitions. He also knew that Blue Boy had to like him if he was going to get close to Lily. Reaching into his bag, he pulled out a slice of apple, and fed it to Blue Boy.

Lily wasn't blind. She knew Taggert was trying to impress Blue Boy. She gave him points for his effort, but really it was either that Blue Boy liked him or he didn't. Luckily for Taggert, her best friend did like him, or at least tolerated him.

They rode for almost an hour, just taking the route along the tree line at the far end of the pasture. The pastures were naturally separated by these tree lines, which made it easier to keep the herds separated.

Lily dismounted and walked Blue Boy around a fence opening. There was a small path that led down to a creek.

She motioned for Taggert to follow her with Diego.

"I never would have seen this," Taggert said, as he led Diego down the slight embankment.

They let the horses drink their fill while they sat down on a nearby log.

Lily took a deep breath. It was nice to be outside, with no destination in mind. "There are lots of places around the property that you have to "know about" in order to find them." She smiled, "Raelynn told me about this pond once…" Lily let her voice trail off.

Taggert wondered why she didn't finish.

Brushing it off, Lily said, "I can't remember where she said it was." In reality, it was because it was a place where Raelynn and Seth made love. Somehow, she didn't think that story would do anything but rile up the chemistry between her and Taggert.

He let it go, even though he suspected there was far more to the story than she offered. Looking for something more neutral, he asked, "So why did you stop barrel racing?"

Lily shrugged, "I guess it was because it was becoming more of a chore than something I enjoyed doing." She picked up a wild flower that grew nearby. "My dad was disappointed, I know, but he never made me feel bad about it."

Taggert gently took the flower from her hand and tucked it behind her ear. She'd taken off her cowboy hat when she got off of Blue Boy so her hair was only held back by the braid. The few wisps that managed to escape caressed her cheek gently in the evening breeze. Taggert longed to be one of them, feeling her skin in a sensual motion.

"I want you to kiss me, Taggert," Lily said, staring into his deep brown eyes. She hadn't meant to be so bold but he just unnerved her with the look in his eyes.

He smiled, reaching up to push the wisps away from her face and tuck them behind her ear, where the flower was. Then, he slowly, very slowly, leaned forward and kissed her.

The kiss was feather light, more like a hint of a kiss. And it left her aching.

When he pulled away, and Lily looked back into his eyes, they were almost black. Desire changed them, making them look dangerous. It was erotic to Lily, seeing the result of buzzing chemistry between them.

Now it was her time to kiss him. She reached up, as he did, but cupped his cheeks in her hands, her fingers rubbing gently across the slight whiskers from the day. "I said kiss, Taggert," she whispered.

Growling, Taggert stood up abruptly, breaking the contact between them. "I know what you said, Lily," he snapped. Then he started pacing in front of her, wearing a path in the low grass that grew there. "You don't think I don't want to kiss you?" he demanded.

Shocked by his reaction, Lily just stood there, staring at him. "Uh," she started, but he interrupted her.

"You think I don't want to tear off your clothes and make love to you right here?" He pointed to the small clearing. "I want you every second of every day!" He paced and fisted his hands, "And I think of you all the time, but you're like a sister to Seth and Ken, and," he seemed to run out of steam, "I don't want to mess this up, with them, or with you."

Still stunned by Taggert's outburst, Lily couldn't say anything for a full minute. She'd never had a man open up and tell her things like that. His honesty was as stimulating to her as his kisses were. She stood up and walked over to where he stood, his back to her, breathing heavily.

Lily ran her fingers around him and hugged him from behind. "I am sorry."

He turned quickly and crushed her to him, breathing in the scent of her hair. She smelled like the first blooming rose in the spring. Her skin was so soft that he thought she was as delicate as a china cup and he was some clumsy elephant stomping around. "I don't want you to be sorry," Taggert whispered into her hair, "I want to know you feel the same way so I don't feel like a lovesick puppy."

Chuckling, Lily thought he was probably the cutest man she'd ever met. She pulled away enough to look up into his eyes, "You are not some lovesick puppy, and I think we both would be stupid if we didn't recognize that there is something powerful between us."

"Well then," Taggert said with a clearer voice, "let's get out of here before I change my mind and rip off your clothes."

Acting dramatically, Lily feigned shock, "Perish the thought," she announced, and giggled as he chased after her.

They collected the horses and walked back up to the pasture.

After getting back up on their horses, they raced back to the barn. Taggert won but only by a few seconds. Blue Boy was older, but spirit had a lot to do with his race.

One of the hands offered to cool down the horses, so they thanked him and went inside to the main house.

As they walked into the kitchen, they came across Seth, Raelynn, Melissa, and John, sitting at the table talking.

"Oh," Raelynn said, surprised by their early return, "we thought you were out riding."

Still flushed from the fast ride, Lily smiled, "We just got back."

Raelynn exchanged looks with Melissa; Lily caught it, but pretended she didn't.

Seth stood up, "Taggert, you haven't met our foreman, John, yet." Then he motioned to Melissa, "Or his wife Melissa. They're good friends of ours."

John stood up and shook Taggert's hand, "Nice to meet you," John said, smiling.

Taggert knew right away that he would like John. He was exactly how Seth described him, a salt-of-the-earth cowboy. As for his pretty wife, Melissa, well she was a bit of a surprise for Taggert, but he just figured John was one lucky man.

The three men jumped right into a conversation about the ranch, which Raelynn discreetly mentioned that they continue elsewhere.

"Why don't we leave the ladies and go into the study for a nice glass of whiskey," Seth suggested. He winked at his wife and led the other two men out of the room.

Melissa came over and hugged Lily, "How are you?" she asked the younger woman.

Nodding, Lily responded, "I'm good, a little busy at work, but that's not a bad thing."

"No it's not," Raelynn piped up.

Straining to hear the men, Melissa kept her ear up until there was no talking in the next room. Then she turned to Lily and asked, "So what's this I hear about you kissing Seth's little, very cute, brother?"

Glaring at Raelynn, Lily sighed, "I see that everyone this side of Houston already knows." She directed the comment at Raelynn, who only shrugged.

Melissa laughed. "Small towns equal very few secrets," she said to Lily.

"Well, it sure doesn't hurt when Raelynn and Mrs. Bentler get together, does it?" Lily asked her friends.

Now Raelynn laughed, "I'm sorry, it's just it reminded me of when Seth and I got together." She patted Lily's hand, "You both look so scared."

Thinking about that word, scared, Lily had to agree with Raelynn's assessment, and spoke up, "I guess that's as good a word as any." She nodded toward Melissa, "But I'll tell you something," smiling she added, "Seth's, very cute, little brother sure can kiss."

That statement prompted a whoop from Melissa and an outright belly laugh from Raelynn.

Melissa recovered first with, "Well, well, little Miss Lily sure did grow up."

Raelynn nodded, "I'm sorry about blabbing," she said to Lily. "I was talking to Rachael and didn't hear Mrs. Bentler, then she added what she saw, and, well, we gossiped."

Lily knew her friend wasn't being malicious so she wasn't mad. After Taggert's revelation during their ride, she had a lot to think about and a decision to make.

"I had lunch with my friends, and they told me all about it," Lily informed Raelynn and Melissa.

Melissa winked, and said conspiratorially, "If you tell me anything personal, Lily, I promise I won't blab about it."

Play slapping at her friend, Raelynn accused, "Melissa Leland, you've been married for less than a year and you're already living vicariously through this young woman."

"Damn straight," Melissa retorted, and they all laughed.

After some more talk, Lily decided she needed to get home.

Taggert, Seth, and John were no longer in the house so she figured they went out to the barn or somewhere else. She said goodbye to Melissa and Raelynn, promising to stop by in a few days for a proper visit, then went outside to her car.

She'd just started it when she saw Taggert jog over to her driver's side door. "I'm sorry, I would've walked you out," he said, breathless from running over.

Placing her hand over his, as it rested on her door, Lily answered, "It's okay, I'll just say goodnight."

Why was she leaving? Didn't she want to be with him? Taggert's mind shot questions in rapid succession.

As if she read his mind, she said, "I'm beat and I don't want to stand here and kiss you when there are eyes watching."

Nodding in understanding, Taggert stepped back, "Okay, goodnight."

She pulled out, watching him in the rearview as she drove down the driveway, smiling like an idiot the whole way.

Chapter 10

The rest of the week flew by, with Lily working twelve hours a day, going home exhausted, but not being able to sleep because Taggert Rhodes haunted her mind. Awake, asleep; it didn't matter, because he was always there.

Thoughts of his body wreaked havoc with hers. Remembering his words, she was soothed into a dreamlike state. She was thirty years old for crying out loud; she should have more self-control over these things.

Friday, after a particularly stressful meeting between a married couple who were now filing for divorce, Lily went home and prayed for silence.

She'd just gotten into the tub when her doorbell rang. "Really?" she yelled sarcastically, to no one.

Grabbing a robe, she slid it over her skin and ran downstairs to see who would dare disturb her.

"This better be good…" she said as she opened the door, her words stopping at the sight of the flowers.

Looking uncomfortable, because there was a woman in a robe at the door, the teenager delivery boy said, "Yes, I have a delivery for Lily Fontaine."

Lily took the flowers, smiling stupidly as she leaned in to smell them. "Would you like a tip?" she asked the young man.

He waved awkwardly, and shook his head no. The glimpse of cleavage was enough of a tip for him.

Frowning at the boy's quick getaway, Lily stepped back inside and closed the door. It was only then that she felt the draft of her open robe and flushed with embarrassment. Hopefully the young man didn't get too much of an eyeful.

Turning her attention back to the flowers, an arrangement of carnations and roses, with a lily set at the center, she looked for a card. It read:

Lily:

I was thinking of you.

Taggert

It certainly wasn't the most romantic note she'd ever received and it wasn't the only time a man had given her a lily, but she was deeply touched. It was simple, and to the point, just like Taggert.

Breathing in the scents of the flowers, Lily was transported to a meadow. She could see herself there, plain as day. Walking slowly, the sun shining down, the tips of her fingers tingling as they brushed the tips of the tall grasses. Then, Taggert was there, standing before her. Then he was walking to her, taking her hands and pulling her so she was flush against his body.

Coming out of the day dream, Lily smiled and ran back upstairs.

Taggert was sitting in the study with Seth, a glass of two fingers of whiskey, next to him. He couldn't drink, couldn't eat, hell, he couldn't think straight; he was too preoccupied with Lily.

This notion of keeping his distance was pure torture.

Feeling restless, he stood up and began pacing in front of the fireplace.

"Something on your mind, Taggert?" Seth asked from behind his desk.

Turning to face his brother, whom he'd grown to care for and respect in a very short time, Taggert felt nervous. "I would like to date Lily," he said shakily.

Putting down the pen he was using to sign some documents, Seth tried not to smile. His brother was actually asking his permission to date Lily...interesting. Sitting back, he tented his fingers and replied, "I though you already were."

Taggert stopped pacing long enough to look at Seth. It was clear his brother was amused by his discomfort. Maybe if it would have been someone else, then he, himself, would've been laughing. But it wasn't someone else, it was him, and he was going crazy.

Seth could see how upset his brother was and knew that, to Taggert at least, this was serious. "I appreciate you letting me know about your intentions." He stood up and walked around the desk. "With her father gone, and me practically warning you off, I can understand your situation." Taking liberties, where he probably shouldn't, Seth answered, "I'm okay with it, but the big question is…is Lily interested in pursuing a relationship with you?"

"She is," Lily announced from the doorway of the study.

After practically breaking every posted speed limit on her way to the ranch, Lily was worked up. She knocked on the back door, but no one answered, so she came in. Raelynn and Seth said she was always welcome here at the house.

She walked through the kitchen and living room, knowing that Seth usually did some work in the study in the evenings. She was going to just ask him where she could find Taggert when she heard their conversation.

Not being able to see Taggert from her position in the doorway, she only heard him asking Seth for permission to date her. It was tough to stand there, rude for one thing, but she really wanted to hear what Seth would say.

Seth turned around and smiled. "Hi, Lily," he said brightly, then added, "I think I'll go upstairs and see if Raelynn needs help putting Hannah down."

Lily smiled at him as he walked past her, then turned her attention to Taggert.

He stood in the room, backlit by the fire in the fireplace. It gave him the appearance of some great warrior.

"You heard?" Taggert asked her, hoping she wasn't insulted by him asking/telling Seth he wanted to date her.

Lily nodded, and stepped further into the room. "I did," she responded, "And did you really think it would make a difference what Seth said?" she asked him back.

Taggert shrugged, "I only bet on sure things, Lily," he stepped closer to her, "if I have to ask Seth, I will," another step, "if I have to go around him so I can see you, I will."

'Well now!' Lily thought to herself. 'There was a bit of a rebel in Taggert after all.'

"Thank you for the flowers; they're beautiful," Lily said softly, taking another step toward him.

He moved closer to her, his breathing more labored from being in near proximity to her. "You're welcome. I meant to deliver them myself, but I was afraid, I'd come inside and..."

She smiled, "And?"

They were a couple steps apart now.

Taggert reached for her, "And..." he whispered before taking Lily into his arms and kissing her.

For someone who'd had their fair share of kisses over the years, Lily felt she was experienced. Taggert's lips on hers, how they moved, how they begged for more of hers; it made her feel like a fumbling teenager. She was actually trembling as his tongue gently parted her lips and gained entry.

Taggert moaned as he deepened the kiss with Lily. Her mouth was warm and tasted sweet, like she did. Like he knew she would. This kiss wasn't like the one the other day, driven by loss, this one was pure electricity between a man and woman.

Was it possible to surrender yourself in just a kiss? Lily wondered. His lips nibbled, sampled, tasted, and feasted on hers. They moved smoothly over hers, as if teaching her what he wanted. Her hands moved up his arms and clamped onto his shoulders. Feeling the muscles pulse under her palms only drove her need higher.

Ripping his lips from hers, Taggert took a step back. Oh, she had him tied up in knots. The way she kissed him was pure madness. His body only thought of its own needs and wanted to be buried deep inside of her.

"Lord, woman!" he said breathlessly.

Lily giggled, "Me?" she asked, astonished.

Coming back to her, he put his arms around her waist, and pulled her to him, "Yes, you."

She could feel him, hard against her, and wondered how she'd missed that earlier. Probably because she was being totally made love to with his kisses. Knowing there was so much more, and feeling this heady, she wasn't sure if she could survive an affair with Taggert Rhodes. But, that didn't stop her from wanting it.

Pushing against Taggert's chest, Lily gave herself some space, to breathe, and to realize where they were. She put her hands up to her throat, gulping in some, much needed, oxygen. "Taggert Rhodes, you certainly know how to sweep a girl off of her feet."

Smiling, Taggert closed the space between them and swept her up into his arms, as if she weighed nothing. "Now, you can say that," he whispered.

Lily was about to kiss him again when she heard a noise from the doorway of the study. There stood Raelynn, smiling.

"This has to stop happening," Raelynn said, her voice full of sarcasm.

Taggert reluctantly put Lily down so she was standing next to him. He kept his hands on her shoulders, not wanting to break the physical contact between them.

Trying to get her mind to kick into gear, Lily finger brushed her hair, then said, "I'm sorry, Raelynn."

Putting her hands on her hips, Raelynn asked, "That's it? That's all you have to say?"

Blank, Lily's mind was blank. What did Raelynn want her to say? "Yes," she said, her voice more solid than she actually felt.

Feeling protective of Lily, Taggert took a step forward, as if he were trying to shield her, "Raelynn," he said, "I apologize if we've offended you by kissing here."

Raelynn bit her lip, "I was teasing, Taggert," she huffed, "I was just going to give Lily a hard time because she didn't come here to see me." She looked at Lily and smiled, "Which used to be the case."

Relief poured through Lily. She didn't want to cause any animosity between Taggert and his family. Walking over to Raelynn, she hugged her friend, and whispered, "We'll choose a more private place next time."

Pulling back from the hug Raelynn whispered back, "Let me know if you need some suggestions," and let Lily return to where Taggert stood.

Without saying anything else, Raelynn left.

Once they were alone again, Taggert and Lily stood in the room, staring at one another.

Lily broke the silence first, saying, "I'm not sure what to say."

He led her over to the sofa and waited for her to sit before sitting down beside her.

"I think," Taggert started, "we can both assume that this is something we'd like to continue."

Nodding, Lily held his hand.

He looked at the doorway, then back to Lily. "I think that privacy is probably something we don't have here either."

"I agree," Lily said. "Would you like to come over to my place?" she asked him, lifting his hand so that she could kiss the tips of his fingers.

Mesmerized by her actions, Taggert simply sat there and watched her. She was unlike any woman he'd ever known. Sighing, he answered, "I can't even begin to tell you how much I want you, woman," he smiled, and added, "But I don't want this quick fling thing."

A little offended, Lily was working up to being mad when Taggert interrupted her, "What I meant was that I want to take it slow. You mean more to me than that."

'Not great, but better,' Lily thought to herself, and nodded.

"How about I take you out for dinner?" Taggert asked her.

Bobbing her head back and forth, Lily pretended that she really had to think about it before answering. After a minute, she smiled and answered, "I think that can be arranged."

Taggert leaned over and gave her a chaste kiss, similar to what he did on the log during their horse ride. He didn't miss the pouty look Lily gave him for his efforts. Chuckling, he tapped her nose, "If I start that again, you won't get out of here."

Lily didn't actually think there was anything wrong with that, but she relented and let him be a gentleman. She stood up and pulled him up, "Walk me to my car, please."

Taggert walked her out, his arm around her waist, and whispered sweet nothings into her ear; how she was pretty as a new born colt and just as sassy; how her hair smelled like fresh picked flowers, growing wild in a field.

From any other man, the words would have sounded like clichés but, from Taggert, they were like spun gold; precious to her.

He walked her out to her car, tucked her inside, and patiently waited for her to roll down the window before leaning in, "Now, you'll have to be a good girl and I'll pick you up at 5pm tomorrow."

Lily patted his cheek, "I think if I were that good of a girl, you might not find me so attractive."

Her words made him so aware, he had to fight to keep from trembling with need. "I'll kiss you goodnight then," he purred and met her lips with his.

It didn't matter that he was leaning in her car, or that she was buckled in, or that this was crazy; it only mattered that he kissed her. He kissed her so hard and fast, that Lily literally thought she was being transported to some other place.

She drove down the driveway a few minutes later, lips swollen from delicious kisses, and a wide smile on her face.

When she turned onto the main road, Lily muttered, "Oh, Lily Fontaine, I think you are in a heap of trouble with that man," but she realized she didn't care at all.

Taggert stood in the driveway, long after the lights of Lily's car disappeared, and wondered how he got here. Smiling, he found he didn't care at all.

Chapter 11

Saturday was bright and sunny, just like Lily's mood. She woke up earlier than she normally did on Saturday mornings, and actually went to the local college to use the walking trail.

The breeze moved just enough that it kept her from sweating too badly. Fall in this part of Texas could be cool or it could hang on to the heat of summer. Lately, it was warmer than normal, so today's coolness was a welcome change.

After her brisk, three mile walk, Lily went home to have a light breakfast and think about her "date" with Taggert.

She called her mom, to check in, and schedule their weekly dinner date for the following Monday. Her assistant, Jennifer, asked if Lily could sign some documents at the office that were completed after Lily left on Friday.

Driving over to her office, grumbling the whole way about "working for yourself meant that you got to set your own hours," Lily opened the door and went inside.

She located the folder and sat down to sign the papers when she noticed the message light on the phone blinking. Pushing the play button, she figured she'd just write down the info from the caller and have it first thing Monday morning. But when the caller started speaking, Lily froze.

"This is Sheriff's Deputy Raymond Spitz from the Bexar County Sheriff's office and I'm looking for a Ms. Lily

Fontaine. Please call me back at 856-555-2300." The message shut off and Lily picked up the receiver to call back the number, a heavy feeling in the pit of her stomach.

She dialed the number and was put through to the operator. After explaining who she was, and who called her, the operator transferred her to another phone.

"Detective Reyes," a voice came over the phone.

Lily sighed, "Yes, my name is Lily Fontaine and I received a call from a Deputy Spitz this morning," she said.

There was the sound of some papers moving, then Detective Reyes came back on the line, "Yes, Ms. Fontaine, we found your business card in the purse of a hit and run victim last night."

Clearing her throat, the heavy feeling multiplying in her gut, Lily asked, "May I ask who the victim is?"

"Yes," the detective answered, "It was a Ms. Claire Walden," the man said directly.

'Oh, sweet Lord,' Lily thought to herself. She'd mailed her card to Claire when she notified her to look for Taggert. "Um," she asked softly, "how is Ms. Walden?"

The detective didn't answer immediately. After a very pregnant pause, he answered, "I'm sorry, Ms. Walden passed away at the hospital this morning."

Lily felt as if her world had just tipped upside down and left her on her head. "Oh Lord," she hissed, trying to keep the tears from pouring down her face.

"So you knew Ms. Walden?" the detective asked, relieved that they found someone who knew her.

Nodding first, Lily finally managed to say, "Yes, I was recently in contact with her to find her son; he's an heir in a will that I'm the executor for."

Her voice actually sounded normal, but Lily felt very abnormal. She was still breathing, and could still see, hear, and taste, but her world was spinning out of control.

The detective only responded with an, "Oh," he then asked, "So you know her son? Do you have a contact number for him?"

Realizing that she didn't have Taggert's cell phone number, she gave the detective Seth and Raelynn's home phone number and explained that the number was his brother's residence.

He thanked her for her assistance and promptly hung up the phone.

Lily sat there, her heart breaking for Taggert. Was it only a week ago that they were there, at his father's funeral? And now, he would need to have another one for his mother. Getting her wits about her, Lily quickly got up and dialed Raelynn's cell phone.

No one answered. 'Dammit!' Lily thought, and jumped in the car, heading over to the ranch.

When she parked her car fifteen minutes later, she found Raelynn in the kitchen, the look of shock apparent on her face.

"They called?" Lily asked her friend.

Raelynn only nodded. "She was such a sweet lady," she said to Lily. "I mean, I know that the circumstances in which she was here were a little odd, but she was a sweet lady," Raelynn brushed at the tears on her cheeks.

Lily walked over and hugged her friend, before asking, "Where's Taggert?"

Sitting at the table, not moving, Raelynn answered, "Out with Seth. They were moving a herd, but I don't know where."

Trying to remain calm in a stressful situation was part of Lily's job description, and, apparently, she needed it today. "Okay then, where's John?" she asked Raelynn.

"In the barn," was the slow answer.

Walking out quickly, she first came across Rachael, who was coming in from the garden.

Smiling at Lily, Rachael said, "Hello, Lily," but then realized something was off, asked, "What's wrong?"

Without missing a beat, Lily responded, "Taggert's mother was killed this morning in a hit and run in Bexar County."

Stepping back, Rachael's face contorted into shock. "Oh my Lord," she whispered, then asked, "Where's Taggert?"

"I'm trying to find out," Lily said, and turned, with Rachael right behind her, to go to the barn.

They found John a few minutes later, who told them that Taggert and Seth were on their way back in and he expected them any minute.

Lily nodded and walked Rachael back to the house.

John knew something bad was coming; the women's demeanor practically screamed it, but it wasn't his place to say. He called his wife, Melissa, and asked her to go over to the main house.

Lily and Rachael had just gotten back to the house, and sat down with Raelynn in the kitchen, when Melissa knocked and came into the kitchen.

Melissa asked, "What's wrong?" She practically ran over after getting John's call. John wasn't one to overreact, so when he said she should go to the house for bad news, she knew it was true.

No one spoke at first, just looked at Melissa. Lily was the first one to speak, saying, "Taggert's mother was killed this morning in a hit and run."

Plopping down in the nearest chair, Melissa was floored. She hadn't met Taggert's mother because she and John offered to watch Hannah during Ken Sr.'s funeral, for Seth and Raelynn.

Even so, Melissa had gotten to know Taggert and considered him family. This was a blow that he certainly didn't deserve, no one did, and it was going to be bad.

Taggert rode down the path towards the barns, just behind Seth. They'd had a good morning, and were successful in transferring a herd to another pasture. He was preoccupied, thinking about Lily and their date later, that he didn't see John come up and talk to Seth. He also didn't see Seth's look of concern.

"Taggert," Seth called to his brother, "let's get back to the house. John said he'd cool down the horses."

Nodding, Taggert dismounted and gave Diego a quick rub on his neck before following Seth toward the house.

He didn't notice that Seth was walking faster than necessary, because he was too busy thinking about Lily. 'Where should they go to dinner tonight?' he wondered to himself as they entered through the back door.

It was only when he was faced with four, very serious looking women that Taggert came out of his daydream. He saw Lily and was going to go to her when Seth held his arm.

Frowning, Taggert looked at his brother questioningly.

"What's happened?" Seth asked Raelynn.

Raelynn started to speak, then closed her mouth.

"Baby?" Seth asked, his fear growing.

Raelynn finally found her voice and said, "I'm fine, Hannah's fine, it's...."

Lily couldn't stand it so she got up and walked over to where Taggert stood. He smiled at her, but it faded when she didn't return it. She took his hands and calmly said, "Taggert, I received a call today from a Sheriff's Deputy in Bexar County."

Nodding, Taggert responded with, "Okay, that's San Antonio area."

"Yes," Lily said, still calm, "they said that your mom was involved in a hit and run earlier this morning."

His nerves were on full alert. "My mom?" he asked, then said forcefully, "She would never hit someone and drive away."

Nodding to him, Lily answered, "She didn't; she was the one who was hit."

'No!' Taggert's mind screamed at him, this wasn't happening. "What hospital is she in?" he asked Lily.

Rachael stood up and walked over to Taggert. She held his arm and said gently, "She's not in the hospital, sweetheart. She was killed."

"What?" Taggert asked, loudly, and backed away from Rachael and Lily. "She's not dead. I just spoke to her yesterday."

Lily had, unfortunately, seen this a few times during her law career. It was never easy and extremely painful for the one who was being informed that a loved one had died. Feeling as she did for Taggert, this felt a hundred times worse. "She's been killed," Lily repeated, and handed him a paper, "here's the contact information for the detective working her case."

It was like a slow motion film was being played out in front of him. Taggert was telling them no, his mom wasn't gone, but they kept insisting. His chest hurt and he was scared, more scared than he'd ever been in his life.

"No," he said again, and left the house.

Seth went after him.

Lily watched from the window as Seth caught up to Taggert. She could see them talking, Seth trying to comfort Taggert, and she saw, with painfully blinding clarity, the moment in which the information sank into Taggert's mind.

She choked back her sobs, hurting for him.

Rachael took Lily by the shoulders and walked her into the study, helping her sit down.

Wanting to forget what she just said, and saw, Lily laid down on the sofa and fell asleep.

Hours later, even though it only felt like minutes, Lily woke up. She went out into the great room to find her mother sitting there with Rachael. They both noticed her about the same time and stood up.

Ginny hugged her daughter, "Are you okay, honey?" she asked Lily.

Unable to process everything quite yet, Lily nodded, but looked lost. "Where's Taggert?" she asked her mother.

Leading Lily over to the sofa, Ginny sat down beside her. "He's gone to San Antonio," she informed Lily, softly.

Lily jumped up, "What?" she asked, upset. "Why didn't someone get me up so I could go with him?" she demanded of Rachael and her mother.

Rachael looked at Ginny, then at Lily, and answered, "Because he didn't want you to go with him." It hurt her to say the words, and, no doubt, hurt Lily to hear them. She and Ginny agreed that honesty was the only possible way in this situation.

"Well," Lily asked, "who went with him then?" She was worried. This whole day was turning into a crazy nightmare.

Ginny felt horrible for Taggert, and her daughter. "No one," she answered Lily's question, "He wanted to go alone."

'Oh, this was not happening!' Lily was screaming inside her head. She remembered, all too clearly, how it felt when her dad died. The pain was horrendous, and she thought it would never go away. Now Taggert would have to go through it, and so soon after losing his dad.

Seth drove Lily home because no one wanted her to drive herself, and he promised her that he would call when he heard from Taggert. John drove his truck so they could leave her car with her.

She called Jennifer and relayed the basic information to her assistant, informing her that Monday was going to be iffy as far as whether or not Lily came into the office. Jennifer understood and assured her boss that everything would be fine.

Lily actually fell asleep quickly once she got into bed. She imagined that it was her body's way of dealing with the stress of the situation.

When she woke up Sunday morning, Lily felt hung over.

She called Raelynn and asked whether or not they had heard from Taggert. They hadn't. So she hung up and sat on her couch the whole day, zoning in and out, watching home improvement shows on the television.

Monday came, and because she hadn't heard from Taggert, Lily decided to go into work. Jennifer was surprised to see her, but had a load of work to keep Lily busy.

The day flew by with Lily working through lunch. Lily even cancelled her dinner with her mother and just went home, in the hopes Taggert would call. Tuesday and Wednesday followed, the same routine. By Thursday, Jennifer was getting worried and voiced her concerns to Lily.

"Okay," Jennifer said, standing in the doorway of her boss's office, "You have to eat, you have to sleep, and," She walked into the office and sat down, "from the look of you, I'd say you're not doing either."

Not that it was any of her assistant's business, but, logically, Lily knew she was right. She nodded, and said, "I know, I'm just waiting."

Getting up to leave, Jennifer commented, "Well, don't wait too long; you don't have much to you as it is."

Lily left the office not long after and was thankful that she had people to care about her. She wondered if Taggert felt all alone and started to cry.

Chapter 12

Two weeks later, Lily was exhausted, emotionally and physically. She was moving on from worry and straight into anger, where Taggert was concerned. Although she understood his situation, not getting in touch with anyone was really unacceptable.

She did understand what he was going through. Over the last couple of weeks, she'd been reliving the time between when she was informed of her father's cancer, and the time he died. None of it, not one second, was anything she chose to revisit. But, in an effort to rationalize Taggert's actions, she tried.

Sitting in her office, studying a brief Jennifer just completed, Lily was engrossed in the legalese and didn't hear the front door open.

Three paragraphs later, she finally looked up and saw Taggert, standing in the doorway of her office, just as he had weeks earlier. Only, this time, he looked awful.

His face was drawn and looked hollowed out; probably from little food or rest. His eyes were red, with bruising underneath, also from lack of sleep, if she were to guess.

"Lily," he said, his voice barely a whisper.

Without thinking about how mad she was, Lily stood up, walked around her desk, and straight into his arms.

Taggert stood there, in her office, holding Lily in his arms, and thanking God that she didn't haul off and punch him. He expected it, after the tongue lashing Raelynn had given him earlier today.

He'd needed time. Time to reconcile losing his mother so quickly, time to make sure her affairs were all in order, and time to figure out what he really wanted. That couldn't be done in a day or two. Hell, he wasn't sure he'd done it in the couple of weeks he'd taken.

Losing a father you never knew was one thing, but losing the mother who raised you and who was your best friend for the majority of your life, well, that was something else altogether. Taggert was, for all intents and purposes, an orphan, and he needed to figure out his next move.

Releasing his hold on Lily, he stepped back so he could see her face. She looked upset and he didn't blame her.

"Thank you, I needed that," he said, his voice raspy with emotion.

Her heart ached for him, but she was still angry. Nodding, she stepped back and retreated back to the chair behind her desk. The distance would help her say what she needed to say.

He came in and sat down in a vacant chair in front of her desk, his hands clasped on his lap. "I'm sorry I didn't call anyone while I was away."

Lily nodded again, wanting to let him vent.

"I guess," Taggert muttered, "I just wasn't ready to lose her."

Emotions poured into her chest, "No one is ever "ready" to lose someone they love, Taggert."

Now, it was Taggert's turn to nod. "I'm not great, but I'm better. And," he added, "I believe I owe you a date."

Even though Lily smiled, she knew it didn't reach her eyes. "Yes, well, I think that we should rethink that," she said as calmly as she could.

"What do you mean?" Taggert asked, another feeling of doom filling his gut.

Lily cleared her throat, "I mean, I've done some thinking too and it's a little too much," she sighed, "for both of us, to take on a relationship right now."

Leaning forward, an edge to his voice, Taggert replied, "You mean, you don't want to take on a relationship with someone who's grieving, and you're mad as a wet hen that I didn't call."

"Pretty much," Lily answered, surprising them both with her candor. "I think you were wrong to shut everyone out when we would have been there to help you."

Taggert sat back, "I see," he said.

Standing up, Lily pointed at him, "I don't think you see one bit." She stalked over to stand in front of him, "I think you are grieving, deeply, which you have every right to do, but I don't feel like getting shut out."

The verbal jab hurt, he wouldn't deny it, but his pride was fierce and wrapped around him like a blanket. "I'll just go then," he said and stood.

Lily stayed where she was until she heard the front door close, then she collapsed into her chair and cried.

"Taggert is back," Seth said to Raelynn when he came out of the office. Since it was at the front of the house, he saw, and heard, the vehicles coming down the driveway first.

Raelynn nodded, but didn't say anything. Their reunion with Taggert earlier was stressful, so she could only hope that his time with Lily went better. But, given that he was back so quickly, she doubted it.

She and Seth were seated at the kitchen table when Taggert came in.

He looked up, defeat in his eyes, although he tried to hide it with a smile.

"How'd it go?" Seth asked, and got a sharp look from his wife for his trouble.

Shaking his head side to side, Taggert answered, "Not well. She's mad."

Raelynn rolled her eyes, "I don't blame her." She glared at the look her husband shot her, "You are free to grieve and hurt, but not shut us out," she said to Taggert. "We're family."

Sitting down at the table, Taggert nodded. "She basically said the same thing, about the shutting out part."

Looking at her brother-in-law, Raelynn felt bad for him, but it was part of making a relationship work. "I have to tell you," he offered, "I was stupid when Seth and I started out, a lot of it was unresolved grief, and I hurt him very badly."

Seth didn't want Raelynn to dwell on that; he covered her hand with his, "But, we made it work, the key word here being work," he added with a smile.

He heard what his brother and sister-in-law were saying, and, rationally, he knew they were right. But, Lily cut into his pride, and he knew, from experience, that those wounds didn't heal quickly.

"Are you willing to work at getting her?" Raelynn asked Taggert.

Not answering, he stood, shrugged his shoulders, and left the room to go up to bed.

Seth held his wife's hand, thankful that they had worked through their issues to find one another. "I love you," he said to her.

Her eyes, moving from the doorway Taggert just left through, Raelynn looked at her husband, a smile on her face, and returned, "I love you too."

Lily was at the running track at the community college, running away from everything in her life, it seemed.

Her pace was light since she was an avid runner, preferring outside on the track to inside on a treadmill. The breeze, the smells, the sun; it all contributed to the experience. She'd just completed her first lap when she heard steps behind her. Moving over, she tried to get out of the way, but, when she looked up, she saw her friend, Ethan, smiling.

Slowing down to a walk, Lily smiled back. She'd come to know Ethan through the local gym and they ran together a couple of times a week. Since her imposed silence from Taggert, she'd been staying away. That wasn't good for her, she knew it, so now she'd taken it up again.

"Where have you been, stranger?" Ethan asked, his smile bright.

Walking at a fast pace, to keep her heart rate elevated, Lily answered, "I've been swamped at work." A half-truth.

Ethan nodded, "So, now that you're back," he smiled, "how about we go out to dinner?"

Surprised by the question, Lily stopped and looked at him. She'd just assumed they were running friends. "As in like a date?" she asked him, to clarify.

"Yes," Ethan answered, "Why not?"

Picking up her pace, Lily answered him, "Why not, indeed."

Raelynn met Lily for lunch two days later. There were two reasons for the lunch date, one was to find out how her friend was, but the other reason was to find out what happened with Taggert. He was mopey and Raelynn cared about him.

They met a little café just off the highway. It was halfway between the ranch and Lily's office.

When Lily walked in, she saw Raelynn right away, and waved in greeting.

Raelynn stood, and hugged her friend, "How are you?" she asked. Looking closely, she could see little smudges under Lily's eyes.

"I'm okay," Lily replied. She sat down, asked the waitress for some water, and then turned to Raelynn, "I'm just tired," she explained.

Understanding, Raelynn smiled, "I assume Taggert came to see you," she opened up right away.

Lily nodded, "He did," she said, "and I told him that I wasn't going to get into a relationship with someone who shut me out."

"He must have felt Deja Vu," Raelynn added, "with the shutting out part." She wrapped her fingers around her cold glass of lemonade, "I told him the same thing."

'Good,' Lily thought, 'maybe then he'd listen.' She thanked the waitress for the water and turned back to

Raelynn, "He took it well." Lily thought for a moment, then said, "Really well, like it didn't matter to him either way."

Raelynn sighed, this was what she was afraid of. "I see," was all she said in return. Things were becoming clearer to her.

They ordered lunch and caught up on things. Rachael went back home, to Wyoming, and was doing well. Ken Jr. and Charlotte sent their thanks to Lily again, for handling things for the estate. Ginny was now getting into some groups at the Senior Center and was trying to rope Lily into volunteer work.

The conversation was bright, skipping around, but they both realized that, underneath, was the simmering issue of Taggert.

Lily refused to let his rudeness affect her friendship with Raelynn. It was really that simple.

"How's Hannah?" Lily asked, trying to keep their subject matter light.

Smiling, Raelynn answered, "In paradise, now that her Uncle Taggert is back." She realized her mistake and grew quiet.

Lily shook her head. "It's fine, Raelynn. He's Seth's brother, so it's fine."

Raelynn wondered if her friend realized just how "un-fine" this whole thing really was.

The next week, Ethan took Lily out on a date. They went up to Pearland and enjoyed a great dinner. The conversation was lively, they had a lot in common, and laughed a lot. The problem was, for Lily at least, that there wasn't the chemistry between them. Not like it was with Taggert.

She chastised herself for even thinking his name. He didn't deserve her time; he didn't even want it. So why was she comparing Ethan, who was sweet and kind and funny, to him?

After dinner, Ethan drove her home. He pulled up in front of her house, and waited for a moment. "I had a great time," he told Lily.

"Me too," Lily answered, and found it was the truth.

She got out and he surprised her by walking her up to her door.

Ethan was nervous, and laughed at himself for being so. "I'd like to know if you want to go out again?" he asked.

Lily nodded, "I would."

He smiled boyishly, then retreated down the steps, going back to his car.

Watching him, Lily smiled, then went inside.

She leaned against the front door once she was inside, praying that she could drum up some more enthusiasm where Ethan was concerned.

Raelynn sat on the porch, with Hannah in her lap, and rocking in one of the big rocking chairs. The evening breeze was a nice relief to the heat of the day. Hannah, for once, was still, lulled by her mama rocking her and humming into her hair.

It was moments like this that were a double-edged sword for Raelynn. She was so thankful to have Hannah, but missed Hailey so much at the same time. Hailey's visit here was too short, as they all were. Raelynn wanted her daughter to live closer and promised to try to convince Hailey of that.

"Hey there," Raelynn heard from the stairs. She turned to see Grace McCormick standing there, all smiles.

Her own face splitting into a wide smile, Raelynn returned, "Hey there, happy bride."

Grace made her way over to the rocking chair next to Raelynn's. She swept a finger over Hannah's cheek, "She's so sweet," Grace whispered.

"She's asleep," Raelynn said in a dry voice, but smiled afterward so Grace knew she was teasing.

Looking over her should, Raelynn asked Grace, "Where's Tavin?"

Dropping her chin, Grace looked deadpan now, "Where else? At the barn meeting Taggert and talking horses and cows with Seth."

"Boys never change," Raelynn offered.

Grace nodded. "So, Taggert...." She grinned and left it open-ended.

Raelynn smiled, "I know, he's a looker."

"Looker?" Grace looked shocked, "He's an underwear model in the making."

Melissa came up to where they sat just then, and added, "Heck, yeah!"

The three of them sat there and chatted for a bit.

Finally, the conversation revolved around to the topic of Lily and Taggert. Grace plied them with questions.

Raelynn shook her head in disappointment. "She's dating that guy, Ethan," she looked at Melissa, "the one she runs with sometimes."

"Oh yes," Melissa said, but sighed, "I'm sorry it didn't work out with Taggert."

Grace looked at them and asked, "Was it promising?"

Shifting Hannah so her arm didn't fall asleep, Raelynn told Grace, "It was like watching fireworks, only between two people."

Melissa smiled, "I've seen that exactly one other time," she looked at Raelynn, "with you and Seth."

"Hey, what about me and Tavin?" Grace asked her aunt.

Chuckling, Melissa answered, "You and Tavin were more like a slow burn; Taggert and Lily were combustible." She pointed to Raelynn, "At least that's what she said, and Mrs. Bentler confirmed."

"Mrs. Bentler saw them?" Grace asked, wanting to laugh at the vision of the ever-proper housekeeper being speechless.

Raelynn corrected, "She saw them together but I caught them kissing, twice," she put up two fingers, "and, I know what I saw."

Grace smiled, and asked, "So what happened?"

Filling her niece in, with bits from Raelynn, Melissa explained that Taggert's mom died and how he didn't call anyone for weeks.

"Oh," Grace put in, "He pulled a Tavin."

Melissa nodded, "Basically."

Shaking her head, Grace said a quick prayer for Lily, "Well, heaven help her then."

They all three laughed since it was a tough road for Grace to hoe when it came to catching Tavin McCormick.

Chapter 13

Taggert worked like a dog. He wanted to prove to Seth that he was an asset to the ranch and he wanted to forget about Lily Fontaine.

A few days earlier, he'd overheard Raelynn telling Seth that she was dating some guy named Ethan.

"Ethan," he mumbled, "What kind of name is Ethan?" he asked his horse, Diego.

The horse snickered, as if to say, "I don't know."

They were moving a herd to a more southern pasture. It helped to let the other pastures grow a little before the cattle fed there and ate all the available grass up.

He was getting to know the ranch well, and was pretty content to be here. It wasn't his own spread, but he was with family. And, that went a long way to soothe his broken heart.

Losing his mom was becoming more of an acceptance now, as he knew it would, eventually. It was tough for him to let go of the thought of her being there.

The last thing she said to him on the phone was, "I saw you looking at Miss Lily; she's a lady, and you have to treat her as one."

He'd laughed it off at the time, thinking that his mom was just busting his chops.

Now, he was rethinking it. He wondered if maybe she was right. Lily said she understood his loss and she did because she only lost her father a couple of years before. But, at the time they spoke, he didn't want to hear platitudes or condolences, he wanted to hold her and be with her.

Every day, he was reminded of what he could have; seeing Seth and Raelynn, happy and in love. He was happy for them, but that tended to mix with a little jealousy. And that, Taggert most certainly didn't like.

He heard the radio go off. It was John, letting all of them know that the last of the herd was in the pasture. His job done, for the moment, he got down and walked beside Diego for a spell.

"Do you think I was wrong?" he asked the horse.

Diego snorted, and knocked his head against Taggert's shoulder, forcefully.

Taggert frowned at the horse, and said, "Fine."

Seth watched his brother and smiled. He remembered a time when he would've talked to his horse too. It was when he and Raelynn couldn't seem to reach one another. It hurt like hell and he wouldn't wish that on anyone.

He rode over to where Taggert was and nodded when Taggert noticed him, "We're done for the day; why don't you go into town?" he suggested.

Shrugging, Taggert answered, "I don't know."

Frustrated, Seth shouted, "You've been moping around the house for weeks now! Please," he pleaded, "go and do something."

Laughing at Seth's dramatic demeanor, Taggert nodded, and answered, "Fine."

Seth was about to turn his horse, Lex, around to head back to the barn, but remembered something. "Oh, I forgot to tell you; we've got about five high school kids coming over tomorrow. They're showing cows at the fair next week and we're going over some things with them beforehand." He pointed to Taggert, "And I'd like you to take the reins on that, excuse the pun."

Laughing, Taggert nodded, "Yes, sir," he answered and did a mock salute.

"Go!" Seth ordered, laughing at his brother's antics.

Just the night before, Seth was on the phone with Ken Jr. and they were discussing Taggert.

Neither of them could understand why, after all those years, their father didn't tell them. It was very strange. Taggert offered a little bit of an answer when he told Seth about the conversation with his mother, the day of the funeral. But still, none of them would ever know why their father did what he did.

Their mother accepted Taggert unconditionally, which didn't surprise either Seth or Ken Jr. She told both of her sons that they were now Taggert's only family and they would do whatever was necessary to keep the family together.

Seth respected his mother, but her position in this delicate and bizarre matter, made him love her all the more. She could have tried to make it very hard for Taggert, could have contested the will, anything; and, yet, she didn't.

Now, it felt like Taggert had always been here. He fit in so perfectly, and his brothers agreed, was just a younger imitation of their father.

As Seth rode back to the house, to his beautiful wife and baby girl, he hoped that Taggert would be able to find such happiness.

Lily finished work and decided to do some shopping before going home. She needed a few grocery staples and had neglected her regular chores over the last month.

She pulled into the grocery store parking lot and berated herself for letting a man take her so far off track. Ethan didn't make her do those sort of things. He was sweet, kind, and generous with his attention. All the things any woman would want.

"Then why don't you want him?" she asked herself as she parked.

The answer came to her mind, but she dared not say that it was because 'he wasn't Taggert Rhodes.'

She was walking into the store when, who should be walking out, but Taggert Rhodes. 'Oh Lord,' she thought to herself, 'give me strength.'

"Lily," Taggert said, nodding his head in greeting.

Stopping in the middle of the doorway, Lily dropped her keys.

Without missing a beat, Taggert bent down and picked them up.

Lily couldn't move; she just stared at him.

Smiling, Taggert didn't know what was going on, only that he felt better at this moment than he had in weeks. But she didn't say anything, just stood there. "Here are your keys." He lifted her keys up and gently placed them into her outstretched hand. "How are you?" he asked hurriedly, trying to spend more time with her.

Getting back her senses, Lily blushed. Just his close proximity had her body shoved into overdrive, her heart racing, and her senses on full alert. "I'm good," she croaked, "How are you?"

Before Taggert could answer, Ethan came up beside Lily. "There you are," he said sweetly and kissed Lily on the cheek.

It was if a bucket of ice-cold water was poured over his heart. Taggert almost choked from the lack of breath in his lungs, seeing another man show Lily affection like that.

"Hi," Ethan said, noticing Taggert. "I'm Ethan." He offered his hand for Taggert to take.

Nodding, Taggert shook the other man's hand and answered, "Taggert."

Lily finally found her voice, "Uh, Taggert is Ken Rhodes' son."

Recognition found Ethan, his smile widening, "Oh, the long, lost son," he said.

Taggert fought the senses in his body that demanded he punch this "Ethan guy" in the jaw.

Wanting to die of embarrassment, Lily dropped her head. This wasn't happening; it wasn't possible to have this much crazy in her life, was it?

Apparently, not catching on to the undercurrent, Ethan said, "Well, it was nice to meet you, Taggert." He put his arms around Lily's shoulder and guided her the rest of the way into the store.

Standing there, watching Lily walk away with another man, Taggert let the anger flow through him.

Seth watched his brother come home and look really pissed off. John was with him, in the barn, and also watched wordlessly, as Taggert saddled up Diego. The horse and man took off like a rocket, the dust trail the only evidence that they were there.

"Well, that's a woman problem there," John said plainly.

Seth nodded, "Yes, sir, it sure is."

John shook his head, "You know the problem with you boys is that you just don't understand women."

Laughing, Seth asked, "And you do?"

Sticking his hands in the air, palms up, he asked, "You've never seen me tearing out of here in an anger so deep or walking around like a lovesick puppy, have you?"

He had a point, to Seth's way of thinking. "You know, you haven't." He turned around to grab another bale of hay, "Maybe I should ask Melissa about the mysteries of John."

John huffed, "I told that woman, plain as day, how I felt and what I needed out of a relationship. And she didn't go running and screaming the other way." He grabbed the next bale of hay to go, "So, I figured she was a keeper."

Seth didn't know if he was more surprised at the fact that John almost sounded like a modern-thinking man, or that he said the word "relationship." It was almost too weird, so he only nodded and continued with their chore.

Taggert rode out to the tree line, where he and Lily rode to on their "date." Was it over a month ago that he kissed her like she was the last drop of water to quench his heart's thirst?

Now she was dating some guy named Ethan who dressed like some sort of suit model and probably knew all sorts of fancy places to take her and knew all the right words to tell her.

Instead of helping to get his anger under control, this train of thought was just riling him up more.

He picked up a rock and threw it. The expended energy did very little to help ease the crushing pain in his heart. It was plain; he missed Lily.

The next day, Taggert met with the group of high school kids for their "lesson."

John explained to him what needed to be done and even picked out a cow for them to practice with.

The kids showed up in a big van, the sign on the side reading FFA (Future Farmers of America). Taggert thought it was a great group and belonged to it at his high school as well.

They filed out, all saying a tentative, "hey," or, "hi." He was about to turn to lead them to the barn when a pretty woman came around the back of the van.

"Hello," she said brightly, extending her hand, "I'm Isabel Carter, the FFA teacher assigned to your group."

They shook hands and Taggert led them to the barn.

It took about twenty minutes to show the kids what the judges would be looking for and what to do to show your animal. They'd probably been told a hundred times during the year, and his little spiel probably bored them, but he did the best he could.

There were a few questions, teenagers thinking they already knew everything didn't provide a great environment for a conversational give and take.

Once everyone seemed done, he walked the group back to their van. The kids piled in and muttered a "thanks." He smiled and walked Isabel around to the front. He opened up the door for her and smiled.

"A gentleman," Isabel said. "What a nice change of pace."

Blushing, Taggert responded, "I'm sure a pretty girl like you gets a lot of attention from the gentlemen around here."

Now Isabel blushed, "Thank you Mr. Rhodes, er, Taggert."

She got in and Taggert shut the door, waving to the group as they pulled out of the driveway.

When he turned around, Taggert came face-to-face with a not-too-pleased looking Raelynn.

"Hi," he said, feeling like he was doing something bad, but not knowing what it was.

Raelynn put her hands on her hips, "Taggert Rhodes, you were flirting with that woman!" she accused.

His anger, still just below the surface, bubbled to the surface. "You know what?" He tried to keep his voice even, "Maybe I was, but Lily doesn't seem to want me so what's the harm in seeing if there might be some woman out there who does?"

The question stuck in the air between them for some very tense seconds.

Recovering first, Raelynn nodded. "You're right, I'm sorry."

Now Taggert really did feel like a jerk. "I'm sorry too, Raelynn. I've got no right snapping at you," he motioned to the barn, "or anyone else around here. You've all been very kind to me."

Stepping forward, Raelynn hugged him. She was pleasantly surprised that he hugged her back. When she stepped away, she saw Seth coming their way, the question in his eyes.

"You go inside; I'd like to speak to Seth," Raelynn told Taggert.

He nodded and did as she requested.

Seth came up to his wife, concerned, "I thought I heard raised voices," he told her.

Raelynn nodded. "Oh, Seth," she tried not to cry, "Lily broke his heart."

Seth suspected as much, given what he and John witnessed the evening before. But, it wasn't for him and Raelynn to meddle in this.

"I know you're going to say, don't meddle," Raelynn read his thoughts, "but I can't stand to see him hurt how you were hurt." She wanted to cry, and was glad when her husband gathered her into his arms.

Rubbing Raelynn's back, Seth soothed her. "I know, baby, but this is their life."

Thinking back to what Grace and Tavin went through, Raelynn was hard pressed to accept what her husband was saying. If it worked with them, then a little meddling might work with Lily and Taggert. Of course, her husband couldn't know anything about it.

She just nodded and walked back to the house with Seth, her mind working overtime.

Chapter 14

The following week marked the beginning of the Brazoria County Fair. It was held just south of Alvin, in the town of Angleton, Texas. It was a pretty big deal for the folks in the county and everyone tried to go.

Taggert heard talk all week from the men about things they wanted to see or people they hoped to run into at the fair.

He wasn't that interested personally, but he heard Seth and Raelynn talking about going. Wanting to fit in with the family, and the community, it was important that he put some effort into going out and meeting people.

The guys on the ranch all seemed to accept him unconditionally, and for that, Taggert was sincerely grateful. Now, if he could only figure out how to get a certain lawyer to talk to him.

Coming in from the barn, he heard John call his name.

"What's going on, John?" he asked as they met up in the middle of the driveway.

John smiled, "That pretty teacher lady, Ms. Carter," he shuffled his feet, "she called me up today and asked if she could talk to you."

Thinking back, he hoped he hadn't said or done anything that would upset Ms. Carter. The kids all seemed okay with his presentation and there were a few moments of…..interest there. He nodded to John as he took the paper with Ms. Carter's number printed on it.

After he showered, he gave her a call.

"Ms. Carter," Taggert said shyly, "this is Taggert Rhodes."

Isabel smiled, "Taggert, I'm glad you called me back." She blushed a little. "I was wondering if you'd like to go to the fair with me on Friday."

'She's sweet,' Taggert thought. "Uh, sure," he answered. "Would you like me to pick you up?" he asked, wanting to be a gentleman.

"Actually," Isabel answered, "I'm going to be here already, helping the kids set up. Can we meet at the main barn, and then we can walk over to the main stage for the rodeo events?" She looked at the schedule, "Say, 6:30pm?"

Nodding, Taggert thought that sounded great, "Sure," he responded. "See you then."

They hung up and Taggert sat there for a few minutes. He couldn't shake the feeling that he was doing something very wrong.

Lily wasn't sure what prompted her to agree to a midweek date with Ethan, but she never should have. Working long hours, with little sleep, meant that she couldn't seem to muster up much enthusiasm about anything, much less a flower show. Actually, she was surprised that Ethan was so into flowers and plants. They cruised the aisles with him oohing and aahing over things she'd never seen. She surely didn't know the names of any of the plants here.

"This one is gorgeous," Ethan held up a small potted plant, "and it would look great in your front yard," he smiled, "right in front of the porch."

'Oh Lord,' Lily mused, 'the man is actually landscaping my yard.' She smiled, despite her internal voice screaming at her to run, run fast, and commented, "It's nice." Although it did look like the last fifteen plants he had picked up.

Taking Lily aside, Ethan smiled and swept a wisp of hair off of her cheek, "You look tired, would you like to call it a night?" he asked.

It was the best suggestion Lily had heard in over a week. "Yes," she said, then added, "I'm sorry, I know how excited you were for this."

He brushed it off, "Sweetheart, you are more important than some silly plants."

Tucking her into his arm, Ethan escorted her back out to his car. They drove back down to Alvin, the ride quiet. Lily just looked outside, watching the large buildings give way to green pastures as they left Houston.

Once Ethan dropped her off, she went inside, waving to him as he pulled out. The last two months had taken their toll and Lily was done.

She went upstairs, peeled off her clothes, and got into bed. It didn't matter that she hadn't eaten since lunch; she just needed sleep.

The next morning, Lily woke up, and for the first time in a while, didn't feel drained. Sheer exhaustion took her through the night and finally gave her the sleep she needed.

Driving over to the college so she could run, she smiled. The sun was shining, it was warm, but the humidity was low, and she felt thankful to just be alive.

She stretched out, taking time for her body to warm up. This was a great release for her, letting all the worries from work slip out of her mind as she ran.

After the first mile, she was actually smiling. She'd just rounded the first turn in the track when she heard the sound of running.

"Is that smile for me?" Ethan asked her, his smile bright.

Lily didn't have the heart to tell him no so she pretended she didn't hear the question, pointing to her headphones. It wasn't right and she knew it.

They ran for the last two miles together, each focused on running.

When they were walking back to the parking lot, Ethan asked Lily, "Would you like to go to the fair tomorrow night?"

Smiling, Lily nodded. She hadn't been to the fair in a few years now, and it would be fun. "Sure," she said and waved to Ethan as she got into her car.

Mid-way through the afternoon, Lily had the epiphany that she'd turned a bend in her emotions. It was sad that Taggert didn't want her, but she would be fine. Not that this "dating" with Ethan was going to go anywhere, but it was a nice distraction right now.

Her assistant, Jennifer, even commented, before leaving, "Good to see you're feeling better."

Lily shooed her out and sat back, thinking about what may have changed.

She just wasn't thinking about him. Not the best way to get over things, but it was what she could do.

A while later, Lily was reading a will she was drawing up for a client when she saw a drop on the paper. Realizing that she was crying, she figured maybe she wasn't really moving on as well as she thought.

The Friday of the fair, Taggert was working in the barn with John. They were going over some paperwork for some new calves and discussing what kind of breeds the ranch might consider bringing on. Taggert's position was diversification, and so far, John and Seth seemed open to the idea.

"So," Taggert asked when they were finishing up, "Are you taking your lovely bride to the fair?"

John nodded, "If I didn't take my woman out to show her off a bit, then I'd be in a heap of trouble now, wouldn't I?" John asked in return.

Taggert chuckled, "I suppose it wouldn't be good."

Snorting, John said, "When you're married, you'll decide how you work with your wife. It's not for the weak, I'll give you that."

Intrigued, Taggert asked, "Why do you say that?"

"Boy," John looked at him pointedly, "In order to be married, you need to be the best man you can. You need to take responsibility for another person completely." He filed away the binder they were working on, "Not financially, although that's part of it, but emotionally." They started walking out of the barn, with John saying, "It's about taking someone else into consideration for the big things."

Nodding, Taggert thought he understood.

John shook his head, "You think you know," he pointed at Taggert, "but you don't. I sure didn't."

Surprised by John's comments, Taggert tried to digest them. He never really thought of marriage in those terms. It didn't help that his parents weren't married. He really had no good example to go off of. He was loved, his mother made sure he knew that, but seeing two people, living together and loving, every day, just wasn't familiar. Seeing Seth and Raelynn did show him a few things. There was a lot of compromising between them.

"You chew on that a spell," John said, then waved as he headed back to his own place.

Taggert walked inside the house and got some water. He was still sitting at the table when Raelynn came in.

She smiled at her brother-in-law, and said, "Hello there, how is your day going?"

Smiling back, Taggert replied, "Good, yours?"

Raelynn sat down, "Mine was good. I worked this morning with Melissa at the office, then came home to a wound up three year old." She sighed.

Leaning forward, Taggert asked, "Why don't you and Seth go to the fair tomorrow night while I babysit?" He pointed upstairs, "I think it's safe to say that Hannah will be okay with me here."

Laughing, Raelynn answered, "I think she's got you wrapped around her little finger," she paused for a second, "but I'd sure appreciate some time out with my honey."

Nodding, Taggert smiled. "I'm sure he'd like that too."

"Are you going to the fair tonight?" Raelynn asked Taggert, knowing full well he was going with Isabel Carter.

Taggert answered, "Yes," he worried that it upset his sister-in-law. "Is that okay?" he asked.

Placing her hand on Taggert's, Raelynn answered, "You are an adult and make your own choices."

She got up and left, Taggert watching her leave, and he still sat there wondering if what he was doing was right.

Lily dressed in some fitted jeans, a light tank with ruffles on the front, and her cowboy boots. Her hair was braided and hidden by her cowboy hat. Looking in the mirror, she was thrown back into memories of her barrel racing days.

The adrenaline would flow like crazy as Blue Boy made his way down the arena, toward the barrels. She could still remember the flip in her belly as they ran like hell toward the finish, just to shave off a millisecond that could make the difference between winning and losing.

Thinking that she should go out to the ranch soon, Lily smiled; Blue Boy probably needed some exercise.

The doorbell rang and she went downstairs. When she opened the door, she wanted to laugh. There stood Ethan, in blue jeans, a plaid shirt in red and white, and a black cowboy hat. He looked extremely out of his element, but tried so hard to hide it.

"Hello there, cowboy," Lily teased.

Smiling at her, Ethan gulped, her outfit made her look like a teenager, and was sexy, to him anyway. "Hello back," he responded, while trying to hide his reaction to her.

She grabbed her purse and phone and they left her house.

Angleton was only about twenty minutes south of Alvin, on Highway 35, so they were at the fairgrounds pretty quickly.

Since it was Friday evening, they ended up parking out in a field, and picking their way through the muddy tracks from vehicles.

Once they were at the gate, Ethan purchased their admission, handed Lily a calendar of events, and asked, "What would you like to do first?"

Biting her cheek in indecision, Lily pondered their options. There was still a good hour before the rodeo portion of the fair started so she smiled and asked, "Would you mind touring the livestock barns?"

Ethan nodded, but Lily could tell it wasn't something he was really enthusiastic about. She looked at it as payback for him taking her to a plant and flower show.

Taggert parked his truck and walked up to the admission booth to get his ticket into the fair. Isabel texted him directions to the barn where she was, if he got there early enough before the rodeo.

Looking at the schedule, he laughed. Rodeo might have been a little strong for the events of the evening. It was

Mutton Busting, which consisted of little kids holding onto sheep. A child's version of bronc riding, he supposed. It was fun to watch though. There was also some barrel racing, he noticed, and he immediately thought of Lily.

How would she look on Blue Boy, racing around the barrels? He imagined that she would be flawless, so in tune with her horse that they moved as one. 'Stop it!' he yelled to himself. It wasn't fair to Isabel if he spent his time with her, but thought about Lily.

Lily and Ethan went into the livestock barn. The familiar smells wafted through the space, animal, hay, and manure, all of it made her smile. Looking at Ethan, she thought all of it made him grimace.

They walked through the wide aisles, looking at the cattle being shown. One of her client's kids was showing a steer here and she stopped to speak to him for a few minutes, wishing him good luck.

"You are very nice," Ethan said to her as they moved down the aisle.

Smiling, Lily answered, "Thank you. He's a great kid. His parents are clients and I can tell they're very proud of him."

Ethan nodded, then asked, "Are you interested in having children?"

Lily had to think about the question for a minute. "Uh," she stammered a little, "I haven't given it a lot of thought."

Taking her hand, Ethan brought it up to his lips and kissed the back of it, he whispered, "You'd make a great mom."

"I, uh," Lily was trying to figure out some kind of response when she almost ran into Taggert Rhodes coming into the barn.

All of the blood drained from Lily's face. She felt like she was caught doing something very bad. Her hand was still in Ethan's and she wanted to yank it loose from his hold. The look on Taggert's face told her he wasn't all that thrilled with running into her and Ethan either.

Ethan spoke first, "Oh, Taggert, right?" he asked Taggert and dropped Lily's hand to extend his own.

Knowing that manners mattered, Taggert shook Ethan's hand, but again, he had to hold back from punching the man. He'd walked toward the barn and saw Lily coming out. It was on the tip of his tongue to say something when he saw the "Ethan" guy with her.

"We were just coming out," Ethan said casually. "Beware of the smell of farm animals," he warned, trying to be funny.

Taggert nodded to Ethan, tipped his hat to Lily, and replied, "It's okay, I'm used to it."

Walking into the barn, Taggert's jaw was tight. 'How could Lily even like that guy?' he asked himself. Personally, he didn't think there was anything wrong with the smell of farm animals. Taggert equated it with hard work and making something of oneself.

"Hey, Taggert!" Isabel hollered to him.

He decided to put Lily and that wuss, Ethan, out of his mind for the time being. "Hi, Isabel," he returned and walked over to where she stood.

Chapter 15

Lily and Ethan found some seats for the rodeo and sat down with their sodas and popcorn. Lily loved this part of the fair, where the kids have some fun. It reminded her of her own childhood and the excitement she felt.

Thoughts of her father permeated her mind, making her miss him even more. She looked over at Ethan, who was on his cell phone…again, and wondered if her father would like him. The truth was, her father would probably think he was too girly.

For Lily, Ethan was safe. Even though her father may not have really liked him, it was nice when he was around.

"I'm sorry," Ethan said, as he ended his call.

Lily looked over and said, "That's okay."

There was some music coming from the stage and helped the crowd's momentum.

Isabel and Taggert found a place to sit in the main stage area. They talked about some of her students' showings at the fair. She thanked him again for giving the kids a demonstration at the ranch.

Waiting for her to sit first, Taggert glanced around. His gaze immediately found Lily. 'Damn it!' he yelled to himself. He would've known her anywhere. Even tonight, with her hair pulled back in a braid and wearing a cowboy hat, he just knew her.

Sitting down, Taggert proceeded to brood.

Isabel chatted nicely about some of the events, not realizing Taggert's mood. He was thankful that she was oblivious, mostly because he was embarrassed by his own behavior.

The emcee introduced the first event, Mutton Busting, and the crowd cheered.

Little kids held on to sheep and rode until they fell off or reached the other end of the corral. Whoever won received a belt buckle. Being as the kids were 5-6 years old, you couldn't help but root for them to hang on. The crowd laughed and whooped and the kids were proud of their efforts.

After that event, the tractor pull started.

"Are you okay?" Isabel asked Taggert.

Shifting out of his mood, Taggert looked over and smiled at her, "I'm good," he answered, but still glared at the back of that Ethan guy's head.

'He's on the phone!' Taggert thought sarcastically. Almost the entire time he was here with Lily, he was on his phone and that annoyed Taggert to no end. If he were to be with Lily, he'd give her all of his attention. "But you're not," he grumbled to himself, "are you?"

Danette Fogarty

Isabel leaned over, "You're not okay; you keep looking at the guy on the phone over there," she motioned toward where Ethan and Lily were sitting.

"I'm sorry," Taggert said.

Smiling, she asked, "Why don't we go and get something to eat and drink?"

Taggert nodded and they got up.

Lily was sitting there, feeling bored. Ethan was on the phone...again, and she wasn't even interested in any of this. She tried to get Ethan's attention but he just put up a finger to say, "one second," and turned away from her. Manners be damned, she got up and left.

The fair was a fun place to be and there was a lot to see. She wasn't going to just sit there while her date was on the phone.

Touring the 4-H buildings, Lily saw all sorts of crafts on display. There were some absolutely beautiful quilts done up, one of them, she knew her mother would love, so she entered a silent bid on it.

She was leaving the craft building when she saw Ethan coming toward her.

"Lily," he said sternly, "you left me."

Surprised by his child-like tone, Lily tried to be calm, "Ethan, I tried to get your attention, but you were on the phone, and apparently, too busy to even look at me."

She was about to move past him when Ethan's hand shot out and grabbed her arm, holding her in place. "We're not done talking," Ethan said in a low, overly calm voice.

Now Lily was not only shocked, but a little afraid. His voice didn't sound calm and he never touched her like that. She was about to say something when Ethan released her arm quickly.

"That's it," Taggert said, and grabbed Ethan. He cocked back his hand, and almost smiled in satisfaction when his fist made contact with the other man's face.

Isabel was shocked, and yelled, "Taggert!"

Ethan doubled over, blood spurting from his nose, "What the hell was that for?" he demanded.

Stepping closer to the injured man, Taggert leaned over and said quietly, so only Ethan could hear, "You ever put your hands on Lily, or any woman like that again, the least of your worries will be a bloody nose."

Grabbing a towel, that was sitting on a nearby table, Isabel pressed it to Ethan's nose, "It's okay," she all but crooned.

Taggert watched her in disbelief as she shot him a glare, then tended to Ethan as if he were the only man in the world.

Lily stood where she was, rubbing her arm, and not believing what she was seeing.

"Come on," Isabel said to Ethan, "we'll take you to the first aid tent."

As they were walking away, Taggert heard Ethan say, "He just hit me," in a whining tone.

Taggert watched them for a bit, a smile splitting his face. 'Well, maybe those two were just meant to be?' he wondered to himself.

Lily stood there, her arm sore, and her pride pretty bruised. Just her luck; she is embarrassed, in public, and Taggert is standing there, with a smug look on his face. Without saying anything, she turned and walked away.

When Taggert turned around, he saw that Lily was walking away. He quickly caught up to her and asked, "Are you alright?"

Refusing to answer him, Lily kept on walking. Unfortunately, Taggert decided to stay with her as she left the fairgrounds. She was upset because she always loved the fair and this was not how she wanted her evening to end. As she passed the entrance, she realized that she'd ridden with Ethan. Now, she could be embarrassed, and sore, and stand there without a ride.

Taggert watched her. He figured she'd come with that horse's ass, Ethan, and would need a ride home. He stopped when she stopped, and watched her get her phone out of her purse. "What are you doing?" he asked, a grin on his face.

Lily looked up, as if just remembering that Taggert was there. Her arm was really hurting now where Ethan had grabbed it, and she was mad. "I'm calling Raelynn and asking her for a ride," she answered quickly.

Gently, Taggert put his hand over her phone. "Now, I think that may be a little unnecessary since I'm right here and I have my truck," he said softly.

"Maybe," Lily answered with a tart tone, "but I don't want to ride in your truck."

Baiting her because he couldn't help himself, Taggert asked, "Are you afraid to be alone with me, Ms. Fontaine?"

The only thing that could even equal Lily's stubbornness was her pride. "I'm not afraid," she shot back at him, a glare in her eyes.

Taggert nodded, "Good," then put his hand at the base of her back, "It's just this way," he prodded and led her to where he'd parked. He felt a little bad because he wasn't escorting Isabel home, but he figured she'd get a ride from her new friend, Ethan.

After he opened the truck door and helped Lily into his truck, he walked around to the driver's side and got in. The temperature was starting to cool so he turned the heat on in the cab and pulled out.

Taggert drove slowly out of the grassy parking area of the fair, and turned onto Highway 35 toward Alvin. He turned up the radio, just a little, to help fill the awkward silence in the truck.

Lily felt so ridiculous; she tried so hard to not draw attention to herself. It did no good to be a good lawyer if you made a mess of yourself. At least, that's what her father always told her. At the scene at the fair, she saw other people watching the exchange between her and Ethan. Then, when Taggert punched him, everyone in the vicinity just stopped and stared. It was humiliating.

"You're mad, aren't you?" Taggert asked her.

Sighing, Lily answered, "A little, yes." She turned a little so she was half-facing Taggert, and added, "But he hurt my arm so I'm a little happy that you punched him."

Her answer surprised Taggert into a laugh. "Well, I aim to please you, ma'am."

Lily moved back so she was staring out the windshield. His words trickled along her skin and made her aware….aware that they were close….and alone. Her pulse started to pick up and her mind raced, wondering what else she could, or would, say.

Taggert would have to be half-dead to not feel the tension between them. He was half tempted to flex his muscles and grunt like a caveman, the impulse to impress her was so great. He came to the first stop light at the outskirts of Alvin, and asked, "Can you give me your address?"

"Oh," Lily blushed, and gave him directions to her place. They were there within minutes and Taggert pulled up in front of her house.

Looking past Lily, Taggert could see the outline of the house, and smiled. It was adorable, just like Lily. Without asking her, he got out of his side of the truck and jogged around to help her out. When he went to take her arm to help her out, she flinched, and Taggert became very angry.

"He hurt you, didn't he?" he asked and examined her arm. There were marks where Ethan's fingers had started to dig into the flesh.

Trying to calm him down, Lily put her hands on Taggert's chest and whispered, "I'm fine. He hurt my pride more than my arm."

Now, Taggert's attention was completely focused on Lily. Her hands were spread across his chest, and they were so close. He wanted to kiss her so badly, but their conversation in her office prevented him from doing so.

Realizing that she was playing with fire, Lily dropped her hands and turned to walk up to the house. She tried, unsuccessfully, to come up with some neutral words of conversation to quell the chemistry between them.

Taggert walked her up to the front door of her house. He noticed the set of chairs on her front porch, and immediately wanted to sit there with her and talk about their days. The vision was so clear that it shook him to his very core.

When Lily turned to face Taggert at the front door, she saw, what appeared to be, fear, on his face. Concerned, she asked him, "Are you okay?"

"I haven't been okay since the first moment I laid eyes on you, Lily Fontaine," Taggert blurted out, without thinking.

Now, it was Lily's turn to be scared. She had absolutely no idea how to respond.

Taggert leaned against the wall, just to the side of the front door, and stared into Lily's eyes. "I think about you all the time," he looked down at his hands for a moment, then back up to her, "and I want to touch you, share your bed, and be with you."

Sure, there were more romantic words said over the years, between men and women. Sure, there were men who could say all the sweet, flowery words that women usually wanted to hear. But, for Lily, Taggert's directness was far more romantic than any words she'd ever heard before. She leaned in and kissed him on the lips. The kiss was slow, and chaste, in comparison to some kisses, but it said all she wanted it to say...that she wanted him too.

"So what do we do?" Taggert asked her, after she ended the kiss.

Lily made a show of pretending to think on the subject. She could see it frustrated Taggert and that made her giggle.

"Woman," he grumbled, "you drive me crazy!"

Frowning, Lily tilted her head and asked in return, "Really?"

Now, he pulled her to him, their bodies flush up against one another, "Yes," he whispered, and kissed her quickly, before saying, "and you know it too."

He kissed her again, only this time, it was with the whole of his heart. Lips touched and fused, tongues darted, as if in a fencing match of emotions.

Lily embraced the feelings running through her chest and the vibrations of need that thrashed inside her whole body. There was a definite battle raging inside of her, only she wasn't sure who was on which side, and who she wanted to win.

When Taggert pulled away, reluctantly, he was out of breath and leaned his forehead against Lily's. "Now do you understand what I'm saying?" he asked, a smile on his lips.

Nodding solemnly, Lily whispered, "Yes, Taggert, I understand now."

She turned to unlock her door. The sound of the key in the lock and the knob opening, echoed into the darkness. Hyper-sensitive, Lily was more aware of everything now.

When the door was opened, she turned back to Taggert and asked, "Would you like to come inside?"

There was nothing in the world Taggert wanted more than to accompany Lily inside her house. But, he also wanted to prove that he wasn't just after her body. "I would love to come inside, Miss Lily," he said, smiling, "but I think we both know I wouldn't be leaving until morning." He took her hand and kissed the back of it. "You deserve more than the neighbors spreading gossip."

He released her hand, nodded to her, and walked off the porch toward his truck.

Lily stood in the doorway, wondering how she could be so mad and so happy all at the same time.

Chapter 16

The next morning, Taggert was whistling as he got Diego ready for the day. He put the horse blanket on Diego's back, then turned to pick up the saddle when he noticed both Seth and John standing close by and staring at him intently.

"Seems like the boy's in a much better mood," John said to Seth, although he kept staring at Taggert.

Nodding, Seth answered, "Seems like maybe he might have had a good time at the fair last night."

John looked serious, and nodded himself. "Looks like maybe a little lady put that smile on his face this morning."

Rolling his eyes, Taggert retorted, "Maybe the two of you should just get to the point and ask me why I'm in a good mood instead of standing there, speculating, and acting like I'm not standing about three feet from you."

Seth shrugged, "Maybe we should ask him why he seems to be in such a good mood." Again, he said it like Taggert couldn't hear him.

About to answer, John noticed a brush in Taggert's hand, and decided, for his own safety, to stop the teasing. "Taggert, you seem in a pretty good mood this morning."

Chuckling, Taggert answered, "Why yes, John, I am in a good mood this morning." He picked up the saddle and put it onto Diego's back. When he pulled the cinch strap around

Diego's chest to secure it, he added, "I happened to run into Ms. Lily and we had a very nice talk."

"Ms. Lily," Seth mimicked, and got a nasty look for his trouble. "What did you and Ms. Lily have to discuss?" he asked his brother.

Taggert stood up and looked at his brother, a mischievous smile on his face, "That," he pointed to Seth, "is nothing you need to worry yourself about."

Seth took a moment before answering, "Ahhh, it was that kind of talk." He elbowed John, "I guess we should let Loverboy get back to work."

As they walked away from Taggert, John said, "Love is in the air and it isn't even spring." He turned around and smiled at Taggert before continuing on his way.

Taggert finished getting Diego set and laughed. He liked both Seth and John, so their teasing didn't irritate him all that much. To his way of thinking, it just meant that they accepted him.

He went out for the morning, with a few of the ranch hands, to check the herds and do a few maintenance things for Seth. It was dirty work and, when he came back in, he was covered in dirt and sweat. The clock said it was early afternoon.

After dismounting from Diego, Taggert spotted John, and asked, "Where's Seth?"

John was working with one of the young colts, transferring him from the barn to a corral, and answered, "He's over doing that crazy skydiving thing he does."

Taggert laughed at John's tone. He nodded and walked out of the barn.

It was a little odd, even to Taggert, that Seth was a ranch owner, but still did skydiving and videography. But, then again, Seth wasn't your average anything. The talks they shared gave Taggert the impression that Seth wanted the roots of his home, but needed the thrill of something freeing. Skydiving, or so Seth said, provided that. Personally, Taggert thought he was crazy, but it was just his opinion. When Seth told him that their father, Ken Sr. did it as well, Taggert couldn't believe it.

He walked toward the house, thinking about his father. The man was a complete puzzle to Taggert and probably always would be. But, it seemed that he cared for Taggert and that went a long way toward reconciling it all in Taggert's mind.

Thinking of his father naturally made him think of his mother. The sharp pain of grief filled his chest. It was almost impossible to believe that she was gone. He would never be able to just call her up and ask her about things. They would never again laugh at the crazy things people did or joke about Taggert's childhood.

"Taggert," Raelynn came out of the house, "are you alright?" she asked. One look at him and she knew he was mentally chewing on something. She knew grief when she saw it and Taggert was still wearing it like a jacket. She knew all-too-well that jacket would lighten as time passed, but you never quite managed to shake it off altogether.

Taggert smiled at his sister-in-law. "Sorry, I was just thinking," he answered softly.

Smiling, Raelynn steered him around the side of the house to a small table on the back patio. It was the same place she came to with Seth on her first visit to the ranch. It was pretty and quiet, the garden on one side, and some beautiful rose bushes on the side closest to the house. Of course, the blooms were gone since it was fall, but they still felt as if they protected this space.

They sat down, Raelynn asking, "Were you thinking about your mom and dad?"

Nodding, Taggert sat down. There was no use in denying it since it was true. He figured there would come a time when he needed to talk about it, and maybe, now was the time. "Yes," he answered, but didn't add any further information.

Leaning back in the chair, Raelynn eyed him closely. "You know, I lost Hailey's father before I even knew I was pregnant with her?"

Shaking his head no, Taggert looked at Raelynn, and could see the reflection of pain flicker in her eyes before it disappeared.

"Yes," Raelynn smiled, "I was this gawky, wallflower in college." She smiled at his reaction of surprise, then continued, "Anthony was this larger-than-life person who swept me up in about ten seconds."

Taggert nodded, interested in the story.

Raelynn was now comfortable with expressing her memories, thanks in a large part to Seth's love, "Oh, I followed him here to Texas for his job and was willing to do whatever he wanted. I loved him so much."

Knowing that Raelynn's husband died, but not sure how, Taggert could see the light dim in her eyes preparing to share that part of her memories. He instinctively reached up and put his hand on hers.

Appreciating her brother-in-law's gesture, Raelynn squeezed his hand before saying, "He was on an oil platform and there was an explosion." She took a deep breath. "Then he was gone."

Taggert ached for her, his brow furrowing.

"Don't feel sorry for me," Raelynn said, "it was his time," she smiled, "and he'd given me Hailey." She sighed at the thought of her daughter, "That was something I wouldn't trade for the world."

Curious, Taggert asked, "And then you met Seth?"

Now, Raelynn's face lit up. The thought of her husband gave her more wonder and love than she could have ever hoped for.

"Well," Raelynn started, "your brother was a complete surprise."

Taggert smiled back, "I'll bet," he responded.

Now Raelynn giggled, "Oh, he just waltzed right up to me and made it clear he was interested."

"Really?" Taggert asked. The picture of Seth walking up to anyone and just being bold, well, it kind of surprised him.

Raelynn spent the next hour telling Taggert about Seth. How he made her feel all the things a woman wanted, needed, and desired to feel.....but how she fought him at every turn. It wasn't something that Raelynn was really proud of; her behavior with Seth was so chaotic in the beginning of their relationship.

Now, she realized it was that she'd never really grieved properly for Anthony and felt she "owed" her dead husband her whole world. She explained to Taggert how it was akin to survivor's guilt, at least according to her therapist, but also told him how Seth never gave up on her. He might have said the words and maybe even left her alone, but that was only in response to her unreasonable behavior.

Raelynn didn't want to cry, but her shame still settled underneath the surface, "I gave him about a hundred times to run like hell from my craziness, but he didn't." She allowed a tear to fall, but smiled, "He just loved me."

Hell, now Taggert wanted to cry. Their love story was full of turmoil and he was actually surprised by that fact. He supposed it was only he and Lily who had these "issues" to contend with.

"Then that crazy bitch ex of his started her crap," Raelynn said sharply.

Taggert's eyebrows shot up. It wasn't like Raelynn to swear. "Uh, do I even ask?" he questioned.

Patting his hand, Raelynn answered, "Let's just save that conversation for a time when you and Seth are both drinking," she watched Melissa wave as she came around the side of the house, "and I am too, preferably."

"What are we discussing?" Melissa asked and patted Taggert on the shoulder in hello, before sitting down.

Taggert answered, "Seth's "crazy bitch of an ex," according to Raelynn."

Melissa nodded, her eyes widening, "Oh yeah, a real ray of sunshine, that one."

They all laughed.

Not being one to hold back, Melissa looked directly at Taggert and asked, "So what's the deal with you and Lily?"

Although Raelynn was used to Melissa's directness, poor Taggert definitely wasn't. He looked like a deer caught in the beams of headlights.

"Uh," he responded.

Melissa shook her head, "You know, you men," she pointed at Taggert, "you guys don't seem to know when you've got the real deal standing right in front of you."

He knew he shouldn't be offended, but Taggert felt his feathers ruffling anyway. "I'm sorry?" he asked, wanting Melissa to elaborate.

Sighing, Melissa leaned forward, her hands clasped together on the table, and said, "Lily is about the most put together woman I know. She's strong, independent, beautiful, and, I might add, one of the most sought after woman around here." She tried not to smile when she saw Taggert's obvious reaction to the last bit, then continued, "And, here she is, wanting you."

Raelynn tried to interject, "Melissa, it's not our place..." but Melissa interrupted her.

"No, he's got to hear this," she said to Raelynn, then turned to face Taggert, "I've only seen the kind of connection you two share one other time."

Feeling defensive, Taggert asked, "And when was that?"

Pointing to Raelynn, Melissa answered, "When I saw Raelynn and Seth together."

That shut up Taggert for a full minute. After what Raelynn just told him about her relationship with Seth, he wondered if it was possible. Their time seemed crazy, but it obviously ended well, since they were married and had Hannah.

"It scares you, doesn't it?" Melissa asked him. She could see the stern look Raelynn was shooting her, but she didn't care. Life was too damn short to be messing around with a good thing. And Lily was about the best thing that Taggert could be offered, in Melissa's opinion anyway.

Taggert looked to Raelynn, then back to Melissa, and said, "Yes, it does scare me."

Shocked by his admission, it was now Melissa's turn to be quiet.

Raelynn smiled, "It's the best kind of scared you can be. It means that you're willing to risk the most vulnerable part of you....your heart."

Normally, Taggert would never even consider having such a conversation with anyone besides his mom....or Lily, if he was going to honest. He nodded to both Raelynn and Melissa, then stood up to go inside.

They watched him go and waited until they heard the screen door close behind him before looking at one another.

Raelynn spoke first, "That was really subtle, Melissa," she said sarcastically.

Melissa sighed. "You know what?" she asked, but didn't wait for an answer, she only said, "I've been with John long enough now that I've learned when it's important to just be blunt."

Raelynn nodded and held her friend's hand, "Well, I told him all about the whirlwind I put Seth through, when we started dating just before that, so he's got a lot to process."

"Listen," Melissa said, "he's like Seth, he's bad ass, but still sensitive."

Laughing, Raelynn said, "Thanks."

Shaking her head, Melissa added, "But he's also got a big heart and loves with all of it." She looked at the house, then back to her friend, "He already feels love for Lily; I can see that."

"Me too," Raelynn answered, "but it's not just him in this, is it?" she asked Melissa.

Smiling, Raelynn offered, "I might as well tell you that Seth told me not to meddle with them."

That made Melissa laugh so hard, she bent over. "Did you tell him that he was crazy to say that?" she asked Raelynn.

Biting her lip, Raelynn answered, "You know, I thought I was doing okay before you busted in on our conversation and started drilling him about his intentions toward Lily."

"Yeah, you just keep telling yourself that," Melissa retorted sarcastically.

Raelynn nodded, "You're probably right. Only, what happens if he tells Seth," she pointed toward the barn, "or John about this little chat?"

Winking at her friend, Melissa responded, "Well, they say Canada is nice this time of year."

The two friends laughed, and moved on to other subjects that were a little less invasive than the question of whether or not Taggert and Lily were going to be able to make their relationship work.

Chapter 17

Taggert went into the house and showered. He was thinking about the conversations with Lily, Raelynn, and Melissa and felt only slightly more settled about his feelings. Sure, he wanted Lily, more than he wanted to breathe, but that didn't necessarily mean it was deeper than just want. Not to mention, if she did or didn't feel the same way.

As he stepped out of the bathroom, a towel wrapped low on his waist, he picked up his phone and dialed Lily's number.

Lily heard the phone ring and jumped up from the sofa. "Hello," she said in a breathy tone.

Taggert smiled, "Good afternoon, Miss Lily."

Just the sound of his voice made Lily's heart skip beats. She felt so solid until Taggert spoke to her or came within a mile of her, then her world tilted. "How are you today?"

"I'm fine," Taggert answered, then asked, "I was wondering if you would come out riding with me later?"

There was nothing that Lily could think of that would be better. "Of course," she replied, "where and when?"

They settled on Taggert picking her up at her house about 6pm, since he was expecting to take care of Hannah for a few hours, so Raelynn and Seth could attend the fair.

After he hung up the phone, Taggert checked his watch and saw it was almost 1:30pm; he needed to get a move on.

After going downstairs and raiding the refrigerator, he went out to the barn and asked a couple of the guys with some help. They jumped in one of the trucks and took off.

Lily was sitting down, waiting for Taggert, by 5:30pm. She'd taken a bath, using the time to shave her legs, and she even used her best bath oil so her skin felt like silk to the touch.

She'd braided her hair intricately, wanting it to look special for Taggert. After he left the night before, she laid in bed and dreamed about him.

The dreams were erotic, romantic, and crazy. They actually gave Lily hope that she and Taggert just might be able to figure all of this out.

He pulled up at 5:55 and Lily jumped off the sofa again, grabbed her hat, her phone, and her purse, before meeting him on the front porch.

Taggert was just rounding the front of his truck when he saw Lily. She was stunning. Some men, he heard, wanted a woman in high heels, a slinky dress, with makeup, and jewelry. He wanted Lily just as she was. Form-fitting jeans, cowboy boots, a light plaid shirt covering a white t-shirt, and her hair braided, ready for riding. To Taggert, that was the sexiest thing she could be in for their date.

He tipped his hat to her, greeting her with, "Ms. Lily, you sure look pretty."

Lily blushed. This wasn't their first date, and yet, she felt nervous. 'That's awareness,' she told herself as she stepped off the porch to take Taggert's hand.

He didn't kiss her, just escorted her to the truck. When she was inside, he shut her door and went around to the driver's side and got in.

Driving the ten minutes to the ranch, neither of them spoke. The radio played some country songs in the background to break up the silence.

Lily stole glances at Taggert as he drove.

His hair was still wet; she guessed from a recent shower. He smelled heavenly, his cologne reflecting him: masculine, and powerful. And, he was grinning, which made Lily wonder what that was all about.

"You can just ask, you know," Taggert said to her as he drove. He didn't dare look over because, if he did, he'd pull the truck over and kiss her until neither one of them could breathe.

Smiling herself, Lily shrugged, "I am just excited and it seems like you are too," she said, as calmly as she could.

Now, Taggert did look at her, and he did pull the truck over. The tires slid a little as they hit the gravel shoulder on the road. He put the truck in park and turned to look at her. She was close now; he could see the sprinkling of freckles across her nose, the sun reflecting off the loose strands of her hair, and how they looked as if they were ribbons floating in the breeze. Reaching up, he cupped her chin with his hand, and said, "I don't think that the word "excited" even begins to cover what I feel about you, Lily."

He didn't use the Miss in front of her name and Lily noticed that first. Then she noticed the look in his eyes. She was sure they matched her own, dark and stormy, filled with need. "Okay," was the only reply she could muster.

With a quick nod, Taggert sat back and pulled the truck back onto the road.

A few minutes later, they were pulling into the driveway of the ranch. In a lot of ways, being here was settling for Lily. She was here almost daily during her teen years, hanging onto every word Ken Sr. told her about horses, the ranch, and everything.

She would come out to ride Blue Boy when she had a bad day, or she was fighting against her parents for teenage independence. There were times when she would follow Seth and Ken Jr. around like a puppy and they would tease her mercilessly about her braces or her frizzy hair.

The memory of coming here just after her father's funeral popped into her mind. She drove out to the ranch, didn't even acknowledge anyone, and saddled up Blue Boy. They rode for hours, the horse allowing her to cry and mourn her father.

"Are you okay?" Taggert asked when he had put the truck in park. Although Lily was sitting next to him, it was clear her mind was miles away.

Jolting out of her memory, Lily pasted a smile on her face, and answered, "I'm sorry. I was thinking about all the times I'd come out here to the ranch."

For some reason, Taggert felt like she was downplaying it, but he'd let it go. She didn't seem upset and he was ready to start their "date."

He jumped out of the truck and went around to the passenger side to open the door for her. As soon as she was out, he took her hand into his and led her toward the barn.

As they passed the house, Lily noticed Raelynn standing in the kitchen window. She smiled and waved at Raelynn, who winked in response.

Their horses were already saddled and ready when Taggert and Lily walked out of the barn.

She walked over to Blue Boy and pulled a carrot out of her pocket. "How's my sweet boy?" she asked as she rubbed his nose.

Blue Boy took the treat and munched on it happily.

"If you give me a gentle ride today, there's more in my pocket for you," Lily whispered into the horse's ear.

Taggert stood a few feet away, watching Lily and Blue Boy. It was plain to see that Blue Boy was her very first love.

Not surprising as most little girls want a horse. There was something special between them and for the first time, instead of jealousy, Taggert felt respect.

They each got up on their horses and turned to head out.

John waved as he worked with a gelding in the corral area.

There was no rush in their ride; it was just two people making their way through time and space, enjoying the fresh air and the company of one another.

Something inside of Taggert settled down. It was like having a warmth move over him, that he couldn't explain, but it gave him great comfort nonetheless. He looked over to see Lily and his breath hitched.

She was sitting comfortably in the saddle, Blue Boy taking his time to walk. The sun only caught the end of her braid, since the rest of her hair was shaded by her cowboy hat, and made it look almost as if it were on fire. Her cheeks were rosy with the fall breeze that whispered across it.

"You look funny," Lily blurted out to Taggert.

They were riding along and his face had changed. He didn't look mad, or scared, or happy, he just looked....different.

Taggert came up to the surface of his thoughts and smiled before answering, "I was just thinking that I'd never seen a more beautiful woman on a horse."

Now, Lily blushed. "Thank you," she returned, then settled in tighter, and prodded Blue Boy into a cantor, leaving Taggert and Diego behind them.

Smiling, Taggert nudged Diego, who was waiting for the sign, to run.

The two of them rode fast, each leaning into the horses for an easier ride.

Feeling the wind rip around her, Lily wore a big smile. Seeing the tree line coming up quickly, she pulled back on the reins, slowing Blue Boy down.

Taggert held Diego back, only a little, to give Lily a lead. She needed the speed and the excitement of it; he understood that since he needed the same thing, at times.

"You let me win," Lily accused him, but was smiling.

He moved so Diego was right next to Blue Boy, and said, "If me letting you win makes you smile like that, I'll be glad to let you win every time."

Those words of his were going to get her in big trouble. 'Yeah right,' Lily told herself, 'you're already in a whole lot of trouble where Taggert Rhodes is concerned.'

Hopping down off of Diego, Taggert turned to help her down off of Blue Boy.

They walked the horses along the tree line for a bit, letting the animals catch their breath.

"Taggert," Lily said as they walked. She'd picked up a long reed of grass and twisted it between her fingers. "Why didn't you stay last night?" she asked.

He stopped and wrapped his arm around her, to bring her body against his, "I told you before, Lily, I won't have your reputation hurt."

Looking up into his brown eyes, Lily wondered if he had any idea of how much of gentleman he really was. "I'm thirty years old, Taggert. I'm pretty sure I can handle any smears my reputation may take."

Growing serious, Taggert's smile fell. "Lily, you are the most important person to me." He looked away for a moment, as if saying the words were difficult, before looking back down at her, "If you hurt, I hurt."

The lump in Lily's throat grew and she had a hard time keeping tears out of her eyes. "Your words are beautiful."

Shaking his head, Taggert answered, "Not as beautiful as you."

That was all Lily could take. She had to kiss him. Reaching up, she pulled his head down so her lips could meet his.

This kiss was no less potent than any of the other kisses they shared, but it was deeper, emotionally, than any kiss Lily ever shared with a man. Her lips were his, her tongue met his, her heart was his, and there was nothing she could do about it now.

Slowly pulling away from Lily, his breath stolen by her lips, Taggert smiled. "Thank you," he said.

Lily closed her eyes and licked her lips, still feeling the heat from his lips on them. She opened her eyes, and answered, "You are welcome."

They continued to walk for a while more, holding hands, but not speaking.

The sun was slowly making its way toward the west as the evening moved in. Since it was almost November, the sun would be setting within an hour or so, and Taggert wanted them settled before then.

He watched for the break in the trees and turned Diego into the tree line.

Lily followed Taggert, not really focusing on their surroundings. Her mind was more occupied with that kiss and his words. She knew that she was falling in love with Taggert Rhodes, probably had been since the day of Ken Sr.'s funeral, but didn't know what to do about it.

A smirk on his face, Taggert led them into a clearing. He waited and knew the moment that Lily saw what he'd done.

As Blue Boy slowed in response to Diego's stopping, and Lily looked up. Her eyes grew wide and she had to stifle a yell of surprise.

They'd come up to where the stream ran through the trees. The same place they'd visited during their last ride together. But this time, it was different, it was....magical!

About twenty feet away from the stream was a bed. Not a traditional bed, this one consisted of hay bales set up in a square. There were thick, wool blankets on top of the hay bales along with pillows and additional blankets. A couple of yards away, there was a fire pit set up, complete with kindling and logs.

Lily looked at the setting, then over to Taggert. "You did all of this?" she asked him.

For the first time, Taggert wasn't sure his plan was a good one. He'd come up with it in his room, thinking that he wanted to do something romantic, but not too conventional. Lord knew, Lily was sophisticated enough; she'd probably eaten at every fancy restaurant between Houston and San Antonio. He wanted to make their time special, like it was the first time they came out riding.

"If you don't like it," he stumbled with the words, "or you think I'm pushing things too fast, I understand."

Dropping Blue Boy's reins, Lily walked over to where Taggert was standing. She took his face into her palms, and looked up into his eyes. "I think," she said with tears in her eyes, "that this about the most romantic thing I've ever seen." She kissed him softly, then said, "And if you weren't willing to make love to me, I was going to have to resort to drastic measures."

Chuckling at her words, Taggert was relieved. "I want you so much, Lily," he whispered.

"I want you too, Taggert," Lily said.

They kissed again, deepening the connection between them. Lily pulled back first, her eyes wide with shock about the setting, and wonder at how much Taggert made her feel.

Chapter 18

They tied the horses up to a nearby tree. They were close enough to the creek to get water and the trees provided a bit of shelter from the wind. Taggert had horse blankets nearby if it got too cold during the night.

When he turned around, he found Lily sitting on the edge of the makeshift bed, smiling.

As Taggert walked toward her, she asked, "How did you do this?"

Pretending to think, Taggert gave her a side glance with a half grin. "Well, I asked a couple of the hands to help me load the hay bales and we brought them out here." He was now standing in front of her, "Then I brought out the blankets and pillows all by myself."

Surprisingly, the bed made out of hay bales was pretty soft. The thickness of the blankets ensured none of the hay poked through. "So you thought you would just make love to me out here, near the creek?"

Taggert shook his head no, "I thought," he pulled her up so she was standing with him, "that, if we both decided," he kissed her hand, "we would make love to each other and not worry about the rest of the world."

Her body and soul were a puddle of molten need at his feet, at least that's what Lily felt like. "That sounds lovely, Taggert Rhodes."

He moved his hands up to gently brace her neck and brought his lips down to hers. He sampled her sweetness before parting his lips and tasting her lips with his tongue.

The passion they toyed with during the ride and the night before, came crashing into them now. Hands reached out, grabbing, touching, sending shockwaves of need through one another. Lips merged into one, creating unimaginable heat.

Lily's eyes were closed, but she was grasping for Taggert's belt buckle. She had to calm herself down to keep her fingers focused on their task. His lips covered hers with bruising need, but she answered his silent demands with her own. She felt her shirt being unbuttoned and released her hands from his belt, long enough to have the shirt slide down her shoulders.

Taggert couldn't breathe and he damn well didn't want to, if it meant not kissing Lily. She filled him up, with some form of life-sustaining energy. He had no thought of anything but her, here, with him, now.

Clothes were peeled off; they giggled when they had to stop kissing long enough to get their cowboy boots off.

Later, they were both naked, and kneeling on the bed in the middle of the tree line. The creek was bubbling by, the birds making their last sounds of the day before settling down for the night, and the only sounds were the sighs coming from Lily and Taggert.

His body was beautiful, Lily thought. He was muscled, from working on the ranch, and his skin was tanned from being in the sun. She ran her fingers along his ribs, closing her eyes as she memorized the feel of him under her fingertips.

Kissing Lily was like drowning in the most delectable way possible. Her skin was so soft, his touch causing her flesh to pebble with goose bumps.

The breeze moved around them as they lay on the makeshift bed, exploring and kissing.

"Are you sure?" Taggert asked her.

Sitting up, Lily started undoing the braids in her hair. As it was freed, it settled down over her shoulders. She lay back down and pulled him to her, "I'm very sure," she whispered.

Moving her over, Taggert positioned himself above her. He wanted to remember this moment, of them being together as one. He gritted his teeth as Lily reached between them and stroked his rock hard shaft, then guided him into her warmth.

It was like sinking into hot lava, with fireworks going off in your head; and Taggert was shaken to the core.

Sighing as Taggert entered her, Lily smiled at the look of absolute shock on his face. He looked like he didn't think it would be like this, but she did. She just knew he would be the other half to her soul, physically.

When Taggert was deep inside of Lily, he began moving. He smiled when she arched up, giving him access to her beautiful breasts. Nibbling and suckling her nipples, Taggert tried to draw out the experience. His motions became more hurried as his body clawed for release.

"Yes, Taggert," Lily whispered into the night air. She could barely make out his features as the sun made its final dip below the horizon. She could see he wanted to let go, but he was waiting for her.

His face tight with need and concentration, Taggert reached down and pulled Lily's legs upward so he was up on his knees. The position allowed him to go deeper into her and draw out her pleasure.

The orgasm came fast and furious, taking Lily into the sweet oblivion on the heels of calling out Taggert's name. She knew he was right behind her, thrusting deeply into her only two more times, before making his own sounds of release and falling down onto the bed, taking her with him.

They laid there, on their "bed" of hay, and cuddled for a long while. At some point, Taggert grabbed another couple of blankets to wrap around them. Nestled in the warmth of his body, Lily allowed herself to drift off into a lovely sleep.

She woke up to the sound of a crackling fire and the smell of food. Sitting up, Lily could see Taggert crouched down by the fire. Since he wasn't facing her, he literally was surrounded by a halo of light.

Taggert heard movement and turned around to find Lily sitting up on the bed. He smiled, "Hey there," he said and went back to sit down next to her. "I thought I'd start a fire and get some food going."

"I'm sorry I fell asleep," Lily said shyly.

Tipping her chin up with his hand, Taggert leaned in and kissed her quickly. "No need to be sorry. I drifted off for a bit myself, exhausted from your physical manipulations, I imagine."

Play slapping his arm, Lily looked around, "Where are my clothes?" she asked. Taggert was dressed in just his jeans but she needed a little more covering than that.

He reached down and lifted the pile of her, neatly folded, clothes up onto the bed beside her.

"You get dressed," Taggert said, "and I'll finish dinner."

He walked back over to where the fire was, giving Lily a little privacy. She got dressed and found an area nearby, in which to take care of her bodily needs, before sitting down next to him near the fire.

Watching Taggert cook steaks on an open fire was like watching a magic show. He expertly flipped the meat, even asking her how she preferred her steak cooked. In another pan, he managed to fry up some potatoes.

After he plated the food and supplied Lily with utensils, she simply sat there and stared at him.

Taggert thought maybe something was wrong, so he asked, "Isn't it good?"

Smiling, Lily answered, "I don't know; I'm still in shock from you cooking steak and potatoes over an open fire and making love to me on a bed of hay in the middle of a forest."

Putting his plate aside, Taggert moved a little closer to her, "No need to be in shock, Lily Fontaine." He kissed her nose, "Just go with it."

Laughing now, Lily repeated, "Go with it," shrugged, and dug into her food.

The food really was fantastic. She'd rarely had better steak, even having dined at some of the more reputable restaurants in Houston. 'Go with it,' she kept repeating to herself.

They finished eating and Lily offered to clean up their dishes. It was the least she could do since he cooked.

After the chores were done, they crawled back up on the bed and laid down, on their bellies, with their heads facing the fire.

"So why did you move back to Alvin?" Taggert asked her. "Seth mentioned you were at a big firm in Houston after law school."

Lily nodded, "I was, and it was exciting and new," she looked over at him, then back to the fire, "but then Dad came to my office one day and asked if I would consider taking over his firm." She played with the edge of the blanket with her fingers. "He wanted to retire, which I couldn't believe, so I told him no, at first. After a few days, I reconsidered and agreed."

Taggert nodded, but looked at her with questions.

"We started working together, and then, one day, Dad just fell ill at work." She was fascinated by the frayed edge of the blanket and worked it with her fingertips.

Remaining silent, Taggert felt she would tell him at the pace she needed to use.

Looking over at Taggert, Lily said, "When Mom and I got to the hospital, he really "looked" sick. The doctor told us it was cancer and he'd found out four months prior to that, but didn't tell anyone."

His eyebrows raised, Taggert realized that keeping the news of his illness from his wife and daughter was the worst thing Mr. Fontaine could have done. "I'm sorry," he said and rubbed Lily's back with the palm of his hand.

"You have no reason to be sorry," Lily responded, the now-familiar anger with her father surfacing, "he was gone in less than two months and we could have had more time with him." She sat up, staring into the fire, "The great Maxwell Fontaine, gone in a flash!"

Taggert sat up; he knew she was upset, but as soon as she told him her father's name, he was confused. "Did you say your father's name was Maxwell?" He asked Lily.

Coming out of herself, Lily processed his question, and nodded, "Yes, Maxwell. Why do you ask?" She looked at Taggert questioningly.

Shaking his head to himself, Taggert answered, "My middle name is Maxwell." He looked over at Lily, "I asked my mother once where she got it from since I didn't see any relatives that had the name, and she told me it was my father's request that my middle name be Maxwell."

Tears fell across her cheeks. "They were so close, our dads." Moving, she turned around so she was seated in front of Taggert, on his lap, with his arm around her. "I'm sure he knew you had his name and I'm sure he was proud of that."

Taggert watched the fire as it played in the darkness, casting shadows and spitting sparks. Much like his mind these days. He wasn't sure if he was mad at the people who knew all the secrets, or just relieved that they were out now so he got to meet Lily. Either way, he wasn't likely to give her up any time soon.

They sat there, watching the fire. Taggert got up once, to put the blankets on the horses, and put more wood on the fire. Neither of them made any move to leave their little place in the woods.

Lily half expected Taggert to ask when she wanted to go back to the ranch so she could go home, but, she didn't want to leave him.

At some point, they fell asleep, wrapped up in one another.

It was very dark and cold when Lily woke up. Her movements must have disturbed Taggert because he moved, and asked, "Are you okay, baby?"

The endearment made her smile, "Yes," she kissed him, "but I'm cold."

Getting up, he piled some more wood onto the almost dead fire, immediately setting it to blaze.

When he turned around, he found Lily had removed her clothes. Smiling, he asked her, "I thought you were cold?"

Looking up at Taggert, Lily smiled, and responded, "Now that I'm looking at you, I'm heating up." She watched as he started unbuttoning his shirt, "Come over here and show me how much you want me."

Taggert threw his shirt to the ground and undid his jeans in record time. Seeing Lily, naked, out in the night like this, did crazy things to his mind and body. He wanted to show her everything.

Seth and Raelynn were sitting in the kitchen, discussing their day, when there was a knock on the back door.

John came in with a worried look on his face. "Hey, Seth," he said, after tipping his hat in greeting to Raelynn, "it looks like we might have a fire out in that tree line off of the west pasture."

Seth looked at Raelynn, who was looking at him, then they both started laughing.

"Did I miss something?" John asked, not amused.

Raelynn bit her lip, then retorted, "Hopefully."

Seth piped up and added, "John, Taggert took Lily out there for a date and said he was going to have a fire going."

Dawning floating across John's face, he shook his head. "Can't these kids just find a bed for Pete's sake?" he asked to the air as he left the kitchen.

Looking at one another again, Seth and Raelynn broke out into another bout of laughter.

Chapter 19

There was a noise in Lily's ear, which she couldn't discern. It was very strange. She opened one eye and was practically face to face with Blue Boy. His big brown eyes, stared blankly at her, as if she was in his way. He nudged her with his nose, to make her move so he could eat....her bed.

Sitting up quickly, Lily looked around, but didn't see Taggert.

She got up quickly, dressed, and moved one of the hay bales closer to Blue Boy and Diego so they could eat their breakfast.

After walking over to the creek, she found a small toiletry bag that, she assumed, Taggert left for her. There was a hair brush, a tooth brush, and even a little tube of toothpaste.

The man was a genius! She thought so, anyway. It didn't take long to get ready since her options were limited, but she brushed her hair out and pulled the blankets off of the hay bales so they could be folded and packed up before returning to the ranch.

Lily heard the sound of a horse approaching and frowned. Both Diego and Blue Boy were still here, tied up, so she doubted it was Taggert. A few minutes later, she smiled when she saw Seth atop Lex, coming toward her.

"Good morning," she smiled.

Nodding, Seth answered, "Well, I guess the coyotes didn't get you, so that's good." He looked around, "Where's Taggert?" he asked Lily.

"I don't know," Lily answered, and heard another sound from her right. Sure enough, Taggert was coming toward them.

Seth chuckled, his brother was being a gentleman and giving the lady, and himself, some privacy. Nodding to Taggert, Seth said, "Raelynn told me to "Get my butt on a horse and come out to bring you two lovebirds in for breakfast," at least that's what I heard before I hightailed it out here."

Taggert nodded, pulling the blankets off the pile Lily created, and stuck them into a big bag. When Seth turned Lex around to head back to the ranch, he finally managed a look at Lily, "Good morning," he growled and pulled her to him.

His lips tasted of toothpaste, Lily thought, and smiled. "Good morning to you too," she answered when he pulled away.

Lily watched him as he saddled the horses. He looked so graceful next to the powerful animals. The fact that Blue Boy even let Taggert touch him, with Lily right there, was surprising still. Diego was used to Taggert's touch and nudged him good naturedly as they went through the motions.

After they were ready, Taggert helped Lily up onto Blue Boy and hopped up onto Diego. He assured her that he'd come out with one of the trucks later and clean up their "bedroom."

As they made their way out of the little cropping of trees, Lily felt a little sad that their night of dreamy lovemaking had to end.

John met them at the barn and was grumbling something about, "youngins and their weird ways."

Lily walked hand-in-hand with Taggert as they made their way to the house.

Once inside, they smelled breakfast, and Lily's stomach growled. She smiled at Raelynn as she stood at the stove and was reprimanding little Hannah for messing up the table when Hannah noticed her uncle.

"Uncle Agger," the little girl screamed, giving her mother, and Mrs. Bentler, a start. She ran as fast as her little legs could carry her then flung herself into Taggert's arms.

Smiling, Lily had pretty much done the same thing as the little girl, so she couldn't really blame her. Taggert's arms were probably her favorite place to be these days too.

Standing there, Lily watched as Taggert gave little Hannah his attention, looking back at her a few times with a silent, "I'm sorry," mouthed.

Raelynn motioned for them to sit down, "Lily, would you like some eggs?" she asked.

Nodding, Lily answered, "Yes, please." She then felt like she was meeting her date's parents for the first time. That was awkward, since she counted Raelynn as one of her best friends.

Mrs. Bentler managed to wrangle Hannah into her high chair, promising the little girl that Uncle Taggert could sit next to her.

Seth came in and walked over to kiss his wife soundly on the lips. She smiled at him, giving him a promise of something more intimate later.

Once everyone was seated, Seth said grace and everyone started eating. Mrs. Bentler watched little Hannah with an eagle's eye, to make sure more was going into her mouth than to the golden retriever sitting underneath the table, named Jack.

Raelynn looked at Lily, and asked, "Did you have a good time last night?"

Blushing, Lily just nodded. Her eyes shot over to Taggert, who was focusing on his food a little too intently.

Mrs. Bentler spoke up, "Now, Raelynn, don't you tease these youngsters about their time."

Seth spoke up then with, "Well, it's more fun that way," and received a motherly look of disapproval from their housekeeper.

Taggert ate quietly, trying not to be the focus of the teasing. He wanted this time with Lily to be special and he feared that Seth and Raelynn's intrusion would take that away. Finally, he looked up to see Lily smiling at Raelynn, and he relaxed. Sometimes, it was easy to forget that he was actually apart of things here. He had to remind himself that Lily had a history with his family that was much longer than his own.

After breakfast, Lily offered to help clean up, but was shooed off by Mrs. Bentler. Since it was Sunday, Seth was going to work at Skydive Spaceland and Raelynn was going to spend the day at the house, with Hannah.

At a loss, Lily made her way upstairs. She figured that Taggert made a run for his room while she was downstairs debating kitchen chores with Mrs. Bentler.

Walking down the hall, she assumed they would put him in the room closest to the stairs. Mostly, to provide him with some sense of privacy since the master bedroom and Hannah's room were at the other end of the hall.

Lily stood in the doorway of the room and watched him as he pulled clothes out of the dresser drawers. "Are you trying to sneak out?" she asked him teasingly.

Taggert stopped, and looked up. He smiled, "Hard to do since I technically live here," he answered and walked over to her to take her into his arms.

"So," Lily smiled, "this is your room."

Nodding, Taggert pulled her farther inside and shut the door before kissing her. This was what he wanted, to keep her to himself.

Kissing Taggert was becoming a sort of addiction for Lily. Her lips literally ached to touch his. And when his lips did kiss hers, Lily felt like she was in a freefall. Almost like how Seth described skydiving.

As Taggert ended the kiss, his body was already begging him to do other things with Lily. He leaned his forehead against Lily's, and said, "I guess I should get you home."

Lily nodded; she really did need to shower and change. "I guess," she said with a sigh, then asked, "how about you bring a change of clothes and stay at my house tonight?"

The thought of spending an entire night, in bed with Lily, again, held great appeal to Taggert. He nodded. "I'll drop you off, do the stuff I promised Seth I'd do here, then I'll come over this afternoon if that's okay."

Smiling, Lily said, "Sounds good." That way she could clean the house and shop for dinner.

They left Taggert's room and went back downstairs. Taggert let Lily know he was going to talk to John quickly, so he knew he was leaving. Lily was left in the house with Raelynn.

"So," Raelynn said slyly, "how was last night?"

Not one to normally kiss and tell, Lily just smiled. She was regaled on many occasions of Raelynn's and Melissa's and even Grace's "evenings" with their guys, so she offered, "It was magical."

Nodding, Raelynn questioned, "Magical?" She winked, and added, "I'll have to tell Seth to up his game."

They laughed and were inundated with Hannah's excitement over her very favorite show on TV.

Taggert came in a few minutes later and said thanks to both Mrs. Bentler and Raelynn for breakfast, then told them he was running Lily home.

As the two of them left, Mrs. Bentler clucked her tongue, and said, "If they aren't married within the next 6 months, I've lost my mind."

Although she chuckled, Raelynn wasn't as sure as Mrs. Bentler about the fate of Taggert and Lily's relationship.

Taggert pulled up in front of Lily's house and his face contorted into anger. He saw, at the same time Lily did, that Ethan was standing on her porch, flowers in his hand.

Lily turned to Taggert, placing her hand on his arm, before saying, "He's obviously here to apologize; let's not make a scene."

Taggert nodded and would do his level best to honor Lily's wishes. But if Ethan so much as put a toe out of line, Taggert would level his sorry ass.

Getting out of the truck, Taggert walked around to open Lily's door, then escorted her up the walk to the porch.

Ethan, looking very apologetic, started with, "I'm just here to say I'm sorry for grabbing you, Lily."

Nodding, Lily said, "Thank you, Ethan."

Eyeing Taggert wearily, Ethan continued, "I, uh, have started dating Isabel, so I'd better get going." He practically shoved the flowers into Lily's hand before giving Taggert a wide berth, "We've got a date and I don't want to be late."

He was in his car, and pulling away, as Lily waved in thanks.

She and Taggert looked at one another for a few moments before bursting out laughing.

"Do I get to keep the flowers?" Lily asked, smelling the bouquet. "I love flowers."

Taggert considered it for a moment, then nodded, and said, "Since they're "I'm sorry" flowers, sure."

Lily winked at him and leaned over to kiss him.

He stepped down off the porch and walked to his truck. Before he pulled away, he gave Lily the longest, most intense look she ever received. The look bored into her soul and opened it up into a well of peace.

After his truck rounded the corner, Lily went inside.

The rest of the morning was spent cleaning her, already pretty clean, house and deciding what to wear. She chose a roast for dinner and put that in the slow cooker with vegetables so she wouldn't have to deal with it until they were ready to eat.

Picking out clothes was an event, with Lily trying on almost every dress she owned. She wanted to look pretty for Taggert. It was one thing to dress for horseback riding, but she was here, in her home, and wanted to blow his socks off.

Finally, she settled on a long-sleeved, print dress that showed off her curvy figure. She loosely pinned up her hair and used the perfume she saved for good occasions. Dabbing on a smidgeon of makeup, just to add color, Lily thought she looked like an actual girl.

The doorbell rang and she flew down the stairs to answer it.

Taggert was at the door, holding a bouquet of roses, and smiling ear to ear.

Lily laughed at the way he held the roses, as if they were some sort of lifeline. The smile was clearly there to hide his nervousness. They shouldn't feel this way, but both of them did.

"I'm the same way," she whispered, as she took the roses from him and kissed him hello.

He tilted his head and asked, "What way?"

Turning to walk into the kitchen, Lily answered, "Nervous."

Watching Lily walk, in a dress, was making him quickly forget about his nerves and focus more on his body's wants. She was a stunner. Gone was the cowgirl with the braids and boots, and here stood the sophisticated woman who made him want to prove his worthiness. Lord, she put him in some crazy atmosphere, where oxygen was scarce and his brain didn't want to work.

As she arranged the flowers, Lily watched Taggert poke around her house. He was curious, but tried to hide it. "Let me give you a tour," she said, when she finished getting the roses into a vase.

They walked all through her house, with Lily pointing out all the things in her house that made it more endearing to her. She was proud of her house, how she'd practically gutted it and redid what she could do, only contracting out what she really couldn't do.

Taggert listened to Lily talk about her house and was impressed with her knowledge. It only proved how independent she was, and how brilliant she was. Not to be underestimated by anyone, Lily Fontaine was definitely her own woman.

When they returned to the kitchen, Lily got out plates and started pulling out the roast to serve it. Taggert offered his help but she said that since he cooked the night before, it was now her turn.

They sat at the dining room table and ate in comfortable silence.

Complimenting her cooking, Taggert asked for seconds. He asked her more about the house and about her law practice, in the hopes of feeling closer to her. This was a whole new level for him and he wanted to do it right.

After they finished dinner, Lily got up to pick up their plates. She said, "I was going to get some dessert, but figured that I'd do."

It was those kind of words that kept Taggert smiling as they went upstairs to Lily's bedroom.

Chapter 20

The next couple of weeks passed in a blur for both Taggert and Lily.

From Mondays to Thursdays, they'd work longer so they could spend Fridays, Saturdays, and Sundays together. Lily would go over to the ranch, to be with Taggert, along with Seth and Raelynn, but they always spent the nights back at her house. It just seemed more appropriate and gave them the privacy they craved.

Those nights were spent with little sleep and making love until they were exhausted.

Midnight snacks in the kitchen, spending time on the porch swing as the sun set in the sky, long walks around Alvin, and sharing the details of their lives with one another made their weekends pass all too quickly.

Lily practically floated into work each morning and even told Jennifer that she was getting a raise.

Even Mrs. Mueller, who usually made Lily insane with the minute details of her never-ending will, got a smile and a thank you said in a dreamy tone.

As she left Lily's office, she commented to Jennifer, "It seems as though Ms. Fontaine has a beau."

Jennifer smiled, and waited until the older woman left before breaking out in laughter.

Two weeks before Thanksgiving, Lily received a call from her mother.

"Hi, Mom," Lily said, as she was packing up her briefcase.

Ginny Fontaine laughed, "Hello yourself, stranger."

Feeling a little guilty, Lily asked, "I've been neglecting you, haven't I?"

Deciding that honesty was best, Ginny answered, "Maybe a little, but I wanted to let you know I've met someone."

The news had Lily stopping what she was doing and sitting stock still. She was surprised by the news, but wasn't upset.

"Don't say anything," Ginny rushed, "I know this may be a blow, but…"

Lily snapped out of her surprise and said, "No, Mom, don't mistake my silence for being upset." She put her briefcase down, "I am not upset, just surprised."

Relief poured over Ginny. "Good," she said. "I was afraid you would think I was betraying your father."

Snorting, Lily answered, "I have no right to say anything of the sort, Mom. You are still a beautiful, and relatively young woman, so you're bound to attract some men."

The tongue-in-cheek remark soothed Ginny's fears. "Geez, thanks, you are too kind."

Lily chuckled, "I actually mean it, Mom. I want you to be happy."

"Like you are?" Ginny asked.

Another surprise, although this one most certainly should not be. "Yes," she answered, "I'm dating Taggert."

Smiling, Ginny asked, "And does he make you happy?"

Sitting back in her chair, Lily took a moment before answering. Taggert Rhodes certainly made her body happy, that was for sure, and, if she were honest, she'd admit that her soul felt safe and loved around him, so she answered, "Yes, he does."

"Good," Ginny replied. "Now, will you come over next week and meet William?"

Now Lily was smiling, "I most certainly will come and meet William."

Now that the news was broken, Ginny wrapped up the call, "I'm going out tonight so I'll let you go," she said, then added, "And please bring Taggert with you for dinner."

"I'll ask him," Lily answered. "I love you, Mom," she said before hanging up.

After hanging up the phone, Lily sat there for a while, and let the thought of her mother dating sink in.

Taggert found Lily at her office, looking very lost in thought. He had knocked after seeing her car still parked there in the driveway. No one answered, so he came in, and found her at her desk. Since she still hadn't noticed him, he was becoming concerned, "Baby," he whispered as he came around the desk, and crouched in front of her.

Lily was so wrapped up in the thought of her parents not being together anymore, that she literally didn't hear Taggert come in. "Oh," she said and cupped his cheek, "I'm sorry, I just got off the phone with my mom." She looked at her clock and realized that she'd hung up with her mom over a half hour earlier.

"Is everything okay?" Taggert asked, worried.

Shaking her head, as if to clear the cobwebs of memories, "No," she started, then said, "I mean, yes, everything is fine."

Confused, Taggert just stayed where he was, searching her face for some clue.

After kissing him, Lily sat back and said, "My mom just told me that she's met someone."

The news took a few seconds to sink in and Taggert started to understand. Change....sometimes it was really hard to accept. He was still trying to adjust to his mother being gone, even seeking the help of a grief counselor, at Raelynn's urging. It did help and he was understanding how grief was very different for every person.

Loving Lily certainly helped. He'd just spent an hour with the counselor talking about his feelings for Lily. He wanted to make sure that he wasn't getting all the feelings of loss mixed in with his new relationship. The counselor assured him that, the fact that he was worried about that, was a sign that he was not misplacing some feelings regarding his mother into a relationship with Lily. It was the first time he admitted, out loud, that he loved her too. The words were kind of scary at first, but now he felt like they were just there.

He'd hoped to profess them to Lily, tonight, over dinner, but now he wondered if that was wise.

"Are you okay?" he asked.

Nodding, Lily waited for him to stand, then she followed him, grabbing her briefcase. "I think I am," she said and followed him out of the office.

They got into their vehicles, with Taggert following Lily, and went back to her place.

Once inside, Lily said, "I'd like to go change, then would you be up for barbeque tonight? There's a great place up in Pearland that I'd like to take you to."

Taggert nodded, and answered, "Sure."

When she went upstairs, he sat down in the living room and looked around. There was one whole wall in her living room that was full of candid photos of her and her parents. He teasingly entitled it, "The life of Lily."

His favorite picture was one of Lily on Blue Boy during one of her barrel racing competitions. The look of sheer determination was plastered on her face and Taggert felt that it represented who Lily really was.

He was still looking at the picture when Lily came downstairs. She was wearing faded jeans, a frilly blouse in a light pink, and black cowboy boots. Her long hair was loose, cascading over her shoulders.

As he turned to look at Lily, Taggert realized he loved all the different sides of Lily. He took her into his arms and kissed her deeply.

Feeling Taggert's arms around her securely, Lily felt like everything would be okay.

"Ready?" Taggert asked, when they ended the kiss.

Nodding, Lily answered, "Oh yeah."

After a beautiful weekend with Taggert, Lily was ready to get back to work. She was tossing around an idea of Taggert moving in with her, but just hadn't gathered up the courage to ask him.

They never specifically talked about the future. Most of their conversations revolved around the immediate present or the past. They both shared stories of their parents and Taggert was eager to hear as much as he could regarding his own father.

The subject simply just didn't come up. Now, she was eager to see if he would consider it. Picking up the phone, she called his cell phone.

"Hello there, sweet Lily," Taggert answered. He now called her sweet Lily and they both seemed to take a shine to it.

Smiling, Lily asked, "I know we usually reserve the weekends but I was wondering if you'd go out on a weeknight with me?"

It was funny because Taggert was thinking the same thing. He had received some mail regarding his mother's estate and a letter from his old boss and wanted to talk to Lily about them. "Sure," he answered.

"Great," Lily said excitedly, then asked, "Is tomorrow night okay?"

Chuckling at her child-like excitement, Taggert answered, "Yes, ma'am."

Lily motioned for her client to come into the office, "I gotta go, but I'll see you tomorrow night."

Her tone meant she was in "lawyer mode" so Taggert just said, "Bye," and hung up. He patted Diego on the neck and said, "I've got a date with Lily tomorrow night." He swore the horse snorted as if to say, okay, so what?

Tuesday morning, Lily made sure she took a change of clothes with her to work. She spoke to Taggert after work the night before and they decided that she would drive out to the ranch, then they would decide where to go.

After she threw in her overnight bag, just in case, she drove to work, singing to the radio at a loud, if slightly off-key, voice.

Luckily, the day flew by and she was able to get out on time. By "on time," that meant before 6pm. Again, she wondered how a person who ran her own business couldn't seem to find a way to get out of work on time.

She drove out to the ranch and pulled into the driveway. The fall air was relatively warm today, with the temps in the low 70's, so Lily kept the windows down.

The smell of cattle and fields filled the air, and made Lily smile. Maybe she would go over and see Blue Boy before she met up with Taggert. After all, her favorite guy had been neglected lately.

Pulling around to the back of the house, Lily parked next to Taggert's truck and went inside.

Raelynn was just inside the kitchen, looking as if she just gotten home herself. "Hey, Lily," she said and hugged her.

"Hey yourself," Lily replied, and helped Raelynn put away some groceries.

After she dodged some questions from Raelynn about her and Taggert, Lily excused herself to go out to see Blue Boy. Raelynn told her that the guys weren't in from the pasture yet.

Lily was on her way to the barn, with a cut up apple for Blue Boy, when she realized she didn't have her cowboy hat. Remembering that she left it in Taggert's truck, she turned around and went back for it. Maybe she'd saddle up her favorite guy and go for a quick ride before the guys got in. Taggert would probably want to shower before they went to eat anyway.

She opened the truck door and was reaching for her hat, when some of Taggert's mail spilled out of it. She would definitely have to talk to him about using her cowboy hat for a mail slot. There was a letter that opened up when it fell out of the hat and landed on the floorboard of the truck.

Picking up the letter, Lily was going to fold it back up, but, for some reason, something caught her eye. She started reading:

Webb Farms

San Antonio, Texas

Taggert:

I know that you mentioned a sizeable inheritance from your father's estate the last time we talked. Since I assume you are still interested in purchasing the 200 acres I offered you last year, I'll assume that you are coming back to this area to finally settle your own place. Should be reasonably priced, but you may want your own person to look over the agreement. Looking forward to seeing you as soon as you get your financial things in order.

Sincerely,

Curtis Webb

Lily was so shocked that she re-read the letter again. It answered a few of the very questions she was going to ask Taggert this evening. He wasn't going to stay here. He was planning on taking the money from his father's estate, and leaving.

Something inside of Lily tore open. It was if she had been gutted with a blunt instrument; it hurt so badly. Tossing the paper back onto the seat, Lily grabbed her hat, and slammed the truck door closed.

She could hear horses coming so knew the men were coming back in. Panic set in and she turned around and got into her own vehicle.

Raelynn was coming out of the house, a look of question on her face, "Lily," she asked, "where are you going?"

Lying to save herself the embarrassment, Lily answered, "I just received a call and have to go back to the office."

"What should I tell Taggert?" Raelynn called out, but the words died in the dust that Lily's car was kicking up.

A few minutes later, Seth and Taggert came inside the house. Taggert was surprised that Lily hadn't arrived and mentioned it to Raelynn.

Frowning, still confused about Lily's departure, Raelynn said, "She was here, but said she got a call and had to go back to the office."

Seth clapped his brother on the back, "That's what you get from dating a successful lawyer," and smiled. He looked at Raelynn after Taggert went upstairs, and asked, "What happened?"

Raelynn shook her head, and answered, "I honestly don't know. She looked so happy when she showed up, and said she was going out to ride Blue Boy. Next thing I see, is her peeling out of here."

She had a bad feeling about this, and prayed that both Taggert and Lily could figure it out.

Chapter 21

That night, Taggert called Lily's house about thirty times, but got no answer. He tried her office, and her cell too, also, with no luck.

On Wednesday, he went over to her office, but Jennifer told him she was at a meeting with a client. When he said he'd wait, Jennifer informed him that the client was from out of town and that Lily wouldn't be in for the rest of the day.

He went home but felt something in his gut that told him something was definitely wrong.

When he didn't hear from her that evening, he went over to her house, but she didn't answer the door. Feeling like a heel, he peeked into her garage but didn't see her car.

Lily went to her mother's house on Wednesday night, to meet her mom's new "friend," William.

She was really looking forward to it, until she read that letter of Taggert's. That paper, and those words, changed everything.

Ringing the doorbell, Lily waited for her mother to answer. Instead, a tall man, in his late fifties, she guessed, answered. "You must be Lily," he said, and extended his hand. "Ginny asked me to greet you while she's in the kitchen."

Smiling, Lily thought that William seemed like a pretty personable guy. She answered, "No problem," and followed him into her mother's kitchen.

Dinner went well. The food was good, although Lily mainly picked at it, and the company was interesting. William left soon afterward, leaving Lily alone with her mother.

"Are you going to tell me what's going on?" Ginny asked her daughter.

Shaking her head no, Lily asked, "Do I have to?"

Ginny sat down next to Lily on the sofa and patted her daughter's hand. "You're not ten anymore, so no," she started, "but I'm here to listen."

The tears started, and Lily leaned over to let her mother hold her. No matter how old a person was, sometimes it was better to be held by their momma.

After her crying jag was completed, Lily wiped her face with the tissue her mother offered. "I'm sorry," she said.

Her mother asked, "What for?"

Taking a deep breath, Lily answered, "For crying and ruining our first dinner together with William."

Ginny waved her hand to dismiss the comment, "Dinner with William was just fine. He said you were very nice, and understood when I asked him to go early so you and I could talk." She smiled at her daughter, and added, "And, never be sorry for crying. I'm your mother."

Taking a breath, Lily tried to find the words. "You know that I've been seeing Taggert Rhodes."

Ginny smiled, "I know you're in love with Taggert Rhodes, yes."

Lily should have known her mother was more in tune with the goings on in her daughter's life, but the comment still surprised her. Pride kept her from responding to Ginny's statement. Instead, she said, "Well, I saw a letter that he received, and it implied that he wasn't going to be staying here." She sighed, "It looks like he's going to take his inheritance from Ken Sr. and buy property out in west Texas and go back to his life there."

Looking at her daughter, Ginny's heart ached. Love was the best and worst thing to happen to a person. It exposed a person to the pain of rejection and loss. "Well," she said, contemplating what Lily said, "I hear words like "implied" and "looks like" so I'm assuming that you haven't discussed this with Taggert to see if it's true."

Shaking her head no, Lily continued, "It just hurt so bad, thinking of him leaving, that I couldn't."

Ginny nodded in understanding. "Honey," she stroked her daughter's hair, "we are all prone to jump to conclusions, but unless we're really communicating, we'll never know what the other person wants."

Lily asked, "Is this what you felt like when you found out Dad was sick?"

Thinking about it, Ginny nodded, and answered, "I suppose so. He could have told either of us, but his wanting to protect us only made it hurt more." She smiled, remembering her husband fondly, "But, I knew he loved me so much that I was willing to forgive that indiscretion."

The answer prompted Lily to ask, "Is that why Rachael forgave Ken Sr. when she found out about Taggert?"

Wanting to be honest with her daughter, but also wanting to respect her friendship with Rachael, Ginny tried to be diplomatic, and replied, "Maybe. That situation was crazy for everyone and, even when we found out, we could see that it was a true hurt for both Ken Sr. and Rachael."

Nodding again, Lily wondered how they handled such a push-pull situation. She imagined that Ken Sr. was very torn between acknowledging his son and respecting his wife and legitimate sons. Nowadays, it wouldn't be any big deal, but then, it was a whole other time.

"The best thing I can say to you, my dear girl, is to search your heart," she smiled, "and then you can be honest with Taggert and figure out what's the best thing for both of you."

Reasonable, Lily thought, but definitely not what she wanted to do right now. Right now, she wanted to hide and pray the pain would just go away. "Thanks for listening,

Mom." Lily stood up, "I'll get going, and you call William and tell him I said he seems to be good for my mom."

Ginny stood, and hugged her daughter, "Thank you, I will."

The drive home from her mother's house gave Lily a few minutes to think. What did she want to do? What if Taggert did want to move back to west Texas? Would he ask her to go with him? Or would he just break it off?

As she got ready for bed, she felt miserable, and very unsettled. Pulling out her phone, she sent out a group text to her Fab 5,

Can we meet for lunch tomorrow, big questions, and I need your help.

Within minutes, responses came back,

Cathy: I'm free,

Anna: Sure, where and when,

Nonie: I can squeeze in some girl time,

Kristin: We're here for you.

Lily smiled and texted the place and time. A while later, when she was in bed and tucked in for the night, she ran through the events of the last two months and prayed that she would come to an answer for herself, and that it was at least close to Taggert's answers.

Within minutes, she drifted off, thinking about Blue Boy and riding through the fields with Taggert on Diego.

The next morning, her phone rang as she was getting ready. Seeing that it was Taggert, she debated on whether or not to answer. Deciding she needed to start dealing with this, she answered, "Hello."

Taggert sighed, "Lily, thank goodness. I was getting really worried."

His tone, which sounded as tormented as hers, softened her tone, "I'm sorry I worried you. I've just been busy."

"You weren't too busy to answer your phone," he snapped. He knew her excuse wasn't the whole truth; he knew that something was wrong. "Why did you leave the ranch the other night?"

Fine, if he wanted to be direct and cross, then she could do the same, "I saw the letter from the Webb Ranch in your truck. I didn't pry, just so you know. It was sitting in my cowboy hat." She sighed, "I know it was yours, but it caught my eye and I read it." Now, she waited for him to respond.

Taggert listened, and could hear her anger, "That was what I wanted to talk to you about the other night," he said defensively. "But you obviously came to your own conclusions and thought pitching a fit was more appropriate."

He was talking to her like a petulant child, and it hurt as much as it angered her. "Fine, I guess I know your answer then, Taggert. You just go back to west Texas and I'll just deal with things here, how about that?" She was yelling by the end of it, but she couldn't help it.

"Maybe I will then!" he yelled back.

Lily hit the disconnect button.

Taggert swore and shoved his phone into his pocket.

Seth was standing a few feet away and heard Taggert's side of the conversation, but didn't comment.

"Dammit!" Taggert spat out the word as he started moving hay bales. The physical exertion necessary for the chore helped him expend some of his anger.

When the bales were rearranged in the barn for winter storage, Seth and Taggert walked out into the main drive. "Do you want to talk about it?" Seth asked.

"I don't know what the hell I want to do," Taggert countered.

Seth nodded, then clapped his brother on the shoulder. "I know it's only about 11am, but I've got some excellent whiskey in my office, and Raelynn is at the office, so why don't we go inside and sample it?"

Eyeing his brother, Taggert actually felt like smiling, "Sounds good," and followed Seth into the house.

Lily arrived at the restaurant first. She couldn't concentrate on work anyway, so she was no use there. Even Jennifer was okay with her cutting out early for lunch, saying, "Take your time," as Lily left.

Within minutes, her four friends arrived. Anna was first, then Kristin, followed by Cathy and Nonie, who arrived together.

Once drink orders were placed, all four of Lily's friends stared at her, waiting for her to explain.

"Thank you all for coming. I'm sorry to pull you away from your own stuff today," Lily started.

Anna spoke first, "Lily, it's fine, what's up?"

For the next half hour, Lily explained the events with Taggert. She gave them everything, except the intimate details, and finally got around to the morning's phone call.

Now, Nonie asked, "Does Taggert understand how you feel about him?"

Kristin nodded, "Yes, I was going to ask if you'd told him you loved him?"

Lily looked around the table, where her four friends were all shaking their heads in agreement. Sighing, she answered, "Well, I never specifically said, "I love you," to him, no."

Cathy shook her head, "How can you expect him to give you consideration if he doesn't even know if you love him or not?" she asked.

This was not what Lily was expecting when she asked for this meeting. She expected her friends to take her side and bash Taggert for being a rude ass. The fact that they didn't made her question her own behavior.

Getting defensive, Lily said, "Hey, I'm not the one who started yelling this morning."

Kristin agreed, "Yes," then added, "but you are the one who ran away when what you really needed to do was get the answers from Taggert, then decide what you each wanted to do about it."

Closing her eyes, Lily chuckled, then asked, "Am I this damn reasonable when one of you has a problem and call a meeting?" she asked, then laughed outright when all four of them nodded yes, enthusiastically.

Patting Lily's hand, Anna said, "The only thing that matters right now, is that you know how you feel about him, and you tell him that." She smiled reassuringly, "The rest will happen and, yes, you may get hurt, but at least you tried."

The advice from her friends made just as much sense as her mother's and was just as wise. The problem was Lily's pride bucked against it....hard. She wanted to be the good guy and make Taggert the bad guy because it wouldn't hurt so much if he left to go back to west Texas. But the truth was, it would hurt even if she wasn't mad, so she was really just wasting her own energy. "Lord, you're right," she said to her friends.

"Now," Kristin said, "I suggest that you get a plan together on how to wrangle yourself up the cowboy you want."

Cathy winked, "I don't suppose you'd consider using some rope and just tying him up to fence post and kissing him until he submitted?" she asked, trying to lighten the mood.

Anna looked mischievous, and added, "Ooh, ooh, wear chaps and spurs so he knows you mean business."

They all laughed.

Lily spent the rest of the lunch trying to make sense of all of it. She wanted Taggert, she loved him, and now she had to figure out how to keep him.

Chapter 22

Taggert was drunk! He slumped down on the sofa in Seth's office. Seth was in a chair, across from him, and not in any better shape. The bottle of whiskey was empty and they were both sitting there, swapping stories about ranches, horses, and women.

"You know," Seth said, then asked Taggert, "I told you about my crazy ex, right?"

Nodding, Taggert leaned forward, "Yup, and Raelynn said something about her too."

Seth smiled, "Oh, Raelynn gave that bitch such a beat down," he said, and laughed.

Shocked, mostly because he couldn't picture his sister-in-law giving anyone a "beat down," Taggert leaned forward and asked, "What?"

Diving into the story about his ex-fiancée, Seth explained how she tried to mess up Raelynn's business, put another guy in the picture to come between them, and actually tried to kill both Seth and Raelynn, "In this very room," he added.

Taggert looked around, expecting to see some evidence of some struggle, four years after the fact. "Wow!" he said.

"Raelynn got free, pinned her to the ground, and started punching her senseless," Seth used his hands to demonstrate as he spoke, "John had to peel her off of Sam."

Laughing at the thought of Raelynn expressing any type of violence, like Seth described, was just too crazy for Taggert to comprehend.

"Yep," Seth said, "and I knew, from that second," he pointed to Taggert to press the point, "that I wasn't going to let her be out of my life."

Sitting back into the sofa, Taggert said, "Yeah, well, if I had a girl who would beat the crap out of people for me, I'd probably keep her too."

From the doorway, Raelynn answered before Seth could, "Well, I'd like to think I had a few more redeeming qualities that Seth took into consideration."

Both men sat up straighter, trying to act sober.

Raelynn had to bite her lip to keep from laughing. "Are we hitting the liquor just a little early today?" she asked.

After a call from Lily, Raelynn decided to come home a little early. It was slow this time of year for their business, so Melissa told her to go home and "kick some butt."

Apparently, she needed to sober up some men before said butt kicking could commence. "Why don't I make us some coffee?" she suggested.

Taggert shook his head to decline, but Seth knew the look his wife was giving him was serious, so he nodded yes.

An hour later, the three of them were sitting in the kitchen. Two cups of coffee did a bit to help Taggert see things a little clearer.

"I came home early," Raelynn said to the men, "because I got a call from Lily."

Taggert's head came up so fast that the room spun a few seconds before settling down. "What's wrong?" he asked, worried.

Raelynn sent her husband a look that told him she loved him, then turned back to Taggert. "Physically," she started, "everything is fine. It's emotionally that things seem to be problematic."

Looking out the kitchen window, he felt like a child who was in trouble. "She started it," he spat out.

Seth snorted, but managed to hold back his laugh, mostly due to his wife's strict look.

Leaning forward, Raelynn asked, "Does it matter who started it, Taggert?"

Memories of his mother flooded his mind, overwhelming him for a moment. She would be ashamed of how he was treating Lily. Hell, he was ashamed of himself, but his pride just kept tripping him up. He didn't want to admit that she had a right to an opinion.

"I want it on my terms," he said to Raelynn, not expecting to voice the thought.

"That's fine, Taggert," Raelynn answered, getting a look of shock from Seth, "Only," she added, "love doesn't work that way. There are two people in every relationship and those TWO people have to work together."

Feeling petulant, he retorted, "That sounds right, but I don't want to."

Her eyebrows raised, Raelynn thought he was acting like Hannah right about now, so she would treat him the same way, "Fine, then you obviously don't love Lily."

The comment had Taggert up and pushing the chair halfway across the room, with his anger. "I love her!" he shouted at Raelynn.

Seth stood, ready to defend his wife, "Taggert, don't take it out on us," he demanded.

Taggert felt awful; he looked to Seth, "I'm sorry," he said, then looked to Raelynn, and said, "I love her so much. I can't breathe most of the time when I'm around her. I look at her and everyone else fades away, as if they never existed. I see her smile, and I'm lifted up onto a level of happiness I can't even express. I feel her in my arms, and my body feels safe, and loved, and crazy, and aroused, and a ton of other things I can't even describe."

Raelynn stood and walked over to her brother-in-law. "Those are beautiful words, Taggert," she rubbed his arm, "but did you ever say them to Lily?" she asked.

"I can't," Taggert said, then turned away from her.

John stood in the doorway to the kitchen, shaking his head. He was coming in to the house to speak to Seth and came in when Taggert was raising his voice to Lynn. If it hadn't been for the fact that Seth was right there, and the words the boy spoke were of love, he'd have taken him out by the scruff of his neck and showed him a thing or two.

He pointed at Taggert, and said, "I stood in this same spot about four years ago now, and yelled at that one," he pointed to Seth, "about not standing up for his woman," he pointed to Raelynn. "I stand here and listen to you wallow about you loving Ms. Lily and yet, you refuse to tell her." He slapped his hat against his leg, "If you love a woman, you damn well tell her. It's up to her, then, whether she wants to stick it out with you, or kick your carcass out." He pointed back at Taggert, "But you tell her, damn it!"

Having said what he felt he had to, John put his cowboy had back on his head, tipped it to Raelynn, and said, "I'll see you at the barn, Seth, when you're ready."

All three of them stood there and watched John leave. No one said anything, only let the words sink in. A few minutes later, Seth went into his office, and came back with a package. He gave it to Taggert and said, "This is for you."

Taggert accepted the package and opened it up to find a letter. As he read it, his mind came up with a plan.

Lily was sitting at her desk, listening to Jennifer close up the office. The afternoon was spent being as ineffective as the morning.

She was about to leave, when her phone rang. Seeing it was Raelynn, she picked up, "Hello," she said, the lack of enthusiasm apparent.

"Well, I've had a better reception from my clients when they owed thousands to the IRS," Raelynn said sarcastically.

Feeling like a heel, Lily apologized, "I'm sorry. I shouldn't have called you earlier either about Taggert. I don't want you and Seth to feel like we've put you in the middle of anything."

Raelynn smiled, "Sweetie, we're family," she said, "if we're not knee deep in everybody's business, then we feel lost."

The joke helped Lily feel better. "So what can I do for you?" she asked her friend.

Winking at Seth, Raelynn said, "Well, the guys are gone for the day; they had to go up to Houston to buy some bull that has great sperm or some such thing."

Lily laughed. "Great sperm, huh?" she asked.

"Exactly," Raelynn replied dryly. "Anyway, they're up there and won't be back until tomorrow so I thought you might like to come out and take a ride on Blue Boy to clear your mind."

That idea held great appeal to Lily. Some time with her favorite guy was probably just what she needed. "Okay," she answered.

Raelynn followed up with, "Don't worry about clothes, I have some here you can wear."

Even better, Lily thought. "Okay, I'll be there in about twenty minutes."

"Sounds good," Raelynn answered, and gave Seth a thumbs up.

They hung up and Raelynn walked into her husband's arms, before saying, "Lord, I hope they don't mess this up."

Seth rubbed his wife's back, and answered, "Love finds a way, and I feel like it's right for Taggert and Lily." He looked over at a picture of his father with him and Ken Jr. It was taken a few years earlier. "Besides," Seth added, "I think Dad and Maxwell would approve."

Raelynn nodded and hugged her husband closer.

Lily left work and drove straight out to the ranch. She would beg Raelynn for an apple or two for Blue Boy, go for a nice, long ride, and then she would come back and try to figure out how to talk Taggert into loving her and staying here. She was sure Raelynn could give her some advice. Heck, she would call Grace McCormick too and see what she did to get Tavin.

After she parked, Lily went inside and found Raelynn, with Melissa and Grace, in the living room. "Is this a party?" she asked the women.

"Heck yeah," Melissa answered, "All the men are gone; we're gonna party!"

Smiling, Lily went over and hugged Grace, "I haven't really talked to you about that wonderful honeymoon, so we'll have to get together soon and chat," she said.

Nodding, Grace answered, "Sure, very soon."

Raelynn pointed to some clothes on a table next to the sofa, "There are your clothes. Have a good ride."

Lily smiled, and said, "Thanks," then grabbed the clothes and went into the downstairs bathroom to change.

A few minutes later, she was on her way to the barn, an apple in hand, and excited to see her favorite boy.

Blue Boy's stall was empty, so Lily walked through the barn, and out behind it. There was Blue Boy, already saddled up.

One of the ranch hands, Chris, came out and nodded to her, "He's all set, Ms. Lily."

"Thanks, Chris," Lily smiled.

Walking over to Blue Boy, Lily rubbed his nose for a few minutes, apologizing to him for being so neglectful. She fed him the apple, while whispering sweet nothings into his ear.

After his treat, Lily allowed Chris to help her up into the saddle. Being in the saddle, the fall breeze blowing, gave Lily a sense of freedom she'd been missing. Being cooped up in the office, she tended to get distracted. She vowed to stop doing that.

Pulling her cowboy hat down low, Lily nudged Blue Boy into a cantor to warm him up. When she thought he was good and ready, she kicked him into a full gallop.

The wind was whipping past her, Blue Boy's mane was flying between them, and Lily felt her troubles start to ease off of her shoulders.

Feeling the excitement of the ride pulse through her made Lily remember her time with Taggert. Them making love, the talks, the smiles, the kisses, the process of them sharing themselves with one another. All those things counted, and, yet she doubted them when she read that letter.

Slowing Blue Boy down, Lily waited until he stopped before she started crying.

Reaching down, she hugged Blue Boy's neck. The tears were flowing for her heart, and the pain of losing Taggert was causing it.

She was so absorbed in her sadness that she didn't notice the tree line was only about ten yards in front of her now and she missed Taggert walking out of it.

Lily sat up and wiped her eyes. When she looked up, she saw a cowboy walking toward her. The sun was behind him, casting a glow behind him. She remembered Taggert looking like that the first night they made love, when the firelight was behind him.

Wiping her eyes again, Lily saw it was, indeed, Taggert who was walking toward her.

Taggert saw Lily riding and was in awe of her. She was going so fast, he was afraid he'd have to jump on Diego and tear off after her. Then she stopped and was crying. It broke his heart, to see the woman he loved, in pain, so he knew he would need to go to her.

"What....what are you doing here?" Lily asked, her voice shaking from crying.

He didn't answer her right away, only kept on walking up to her. When he was just beside Blue Boy, he reached out to scratch the horse's ear before extending his hand up to Lily.

Lily knew his hand would be an emotional lifeline for her, so she took it and let him help her down.

Watching Lily as she slid down off the horse, Taggert waited until her feet were on the ground before saying, "I needed you," he whispered, and kissed her forehead. He pulled back enough to look into her eyes and added, "And I want to tell you something." His heart was pounding from nerves and his love for her.

Looking up at Taggert, Lily could barely breathe. "What do you want to tell me?" she asked.

Rubbing his thumb across Lily's soft cheek, Taggert replied, "I wanted to tell you that I'm a prideful ass and I'm in love with you." He kissed her nose, "And I want to tell you that I won't leave you; I'm here, with you, for you, and will be until I take my last breath on this earth."

The tears started to run down her cheeks again, only these weren't tears of sadness, they were tears of joy. The joy of knowing that the man she loved, loved her just as much. "I love you too, and, I guess, we're both prideful asses."

Taggert's head fell back as he laughed. "I think then, we're exactly where we are meant to be then."

Lily watched his brown eyes, and knew he was telling her what was in his heart. She took in the sight of the sun setting in the west, the breeze blowing softly, the sound of Blue Boy as he was restless behind her, and the sight of the most beautiful cowboy in the whole world in front of her.

Kissing Lily once more, Taggert sealed the deal with his lips, telling his love with everything he couldn't say with words. When he released her, he bent down, and opened a box. There was a ring inside. Lily stood there in shock.

"This ring was the ring that my father gave Rachael when they got engaged," Taggert said, with a shaky voice. "She sent it to me a week ago, through Seth, with a letter." He took out the piece of paper and began to read it:

Dear Taggert:

I know this may seem very odd, my sending you a ring. I watched you and Lily very closely while at your father's funeral and for the days following. I'm convinced, in my heart, that your father and Maxwell, must have known that you and Lily would end up together. Before he passed away, your father asked me to give you this engagement ring. He said that you would find your true love, just as he found his (in me) and you probably would fumble with it, just as he did. My sincerest wish is that you and Lily find the love your father and I found.

My love and wishes,

Rachael

Taggert's voice shook again as he read the letter to Lily. He refolded the letter and put it in his pocket, took the ring out of the box, and slid it on Lily's finger. "I know that I'm not a prince, I'm just a man, but I promise to do everything I can to make a life with you filled with happiness."

Lily's eyes were filled with tears so it took her a few moments to see Taggert clearly. "I can't think of anything I'd love more," she answered.

An hour later, Lily and Taggert rode back to the ranch. As they hopped down from the horses, they saw Seth and

Raelynn, Grace and Tavin, along with Melissa and John, standing there, waiting.

John nodded to the couple and said, "I guess she didn't kick his carcass out," and everyone laughed.

Amidst hugs and kisses and congratulations, Lily thought, as far as happy endings went....this one was pretty good.

(To my own Daddy, I know that you are proud of me and my books, and I know you are looking down from Heaven right now, laughing at my jokes. I miss you!)

www.ingramcontent.com/pod-product-compliance
Lightning Source LLC
Chambersburg PA
CBHW060737050426
42449CB00008B/1253